Simply Irresistible

Simply
Irresistible

*Attract the best of everything
in your work an· career!*

Diana Davin

Blossie's Books
www.blossiesbooks.com

Published by Blossie's Books
1-201-450-3654
E-mail: info@blossiesbooks.com
www.blossiesbooks.com
ISBN 13: 978-1-891019-48-7

Also by Diana Davin

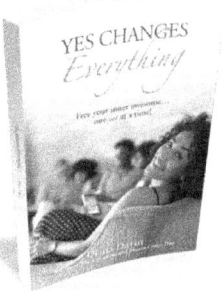

Make this book your own

Everyone comes to a book like this at different points. Make this book your own by looking for the ideas that make the most sense for you. Then, go be awesome by using these ideas when, how, and where they fit your unique and beautiful life.

Disclaimer

Blossie's Books aim to help you open your mind and eyes to an amazing, high potential future and build the life you want. Your results, however, are your responsibility. Blossiesbooks.com does not provide legal, health, or financial advice and does not guarantee the results obtained by readers of its books, blogs, website, or any other materials.

Privacy

As always, the names I use in my stories have been changed to protect the privacy of my friends and clients.

Blossie's Books
Go be awesome
@ work!

Welcome to Blossie @work!

Work today has changed — a lot. Our true lives (families, kitchens, basements, cars)... are newly visible and accepted. Our in-person jobs in restaurants, gyms, grocery and retail stores can also get a lift from a new outlook of flexibility, kindness, respect, generosity, and support.

So, maybe more should change too...maybe it's time to see success as something bigger than just money and power. This would also be a great time to ditch productivity at the expense of creativity, winning by creating a loser, and competing instead of cooperating.

Because in this new world of work, we *can* succeed and still be gracious and grateful and giving. Instead of climbing over other people, we can take them with us. We can excel <u>and</u> enjoy the work we do and the people we do it with and for.

As always, beautiful someone, I am hopeful.

Now, let's go be awesome — at work!

Contents

"Advance confidently
in the direction of your
dreams and endeavor
to live the life that
you have imagined,
and you will meet with
a success unexpected
in common hours."

— Henry David Thoreau
Walden

The Story of *Simply Irresistible*

Being irresistible has the power
to put us in front of the right people
and shortlisted for the best opportunities.

After working with Jon for a year, I started calling him "Jon the Irresistible" because everywhere he went, people were just drawn to him.

When he talked — any time, about anything — everyone stopped what they were doing to listen. And if he needed literally anything, people rushed in to help. Jon knew how to encourage everyone to share their ideas and ask questions, and never let them leave feeling stupid or embarrassed. "I feel like a genius around him," one said.

This fascinated me! What was it about Jon that he could make his coworkers feel so relaxed and comfortable?

In the last 10 years, I've met other people like Jon, irresistible people who seem to genuinely like and respect their coworkers and are liked and respected in return.

Like Jon, they make people feel valued and included. They have other great qualities too: they're cool under pressure, the go-to person in tough situations. They stop to think before they talk or click Send, especially in high-stakes situations.

These irresistible people are curious about ideas. They pay close attention to other people. They know when to stop talking and start listening. They use positive body language to show they're totally focused on a conversation with someone,

1

sending the clear message, "Right now, there's nothing more important going on in my workday than talking to you." They ask really good questions, and their timing is spot-on.

Since one of the best sounds someone can hear is their own name, irresistible people don't allow themselves excuses like, "I'm bad with names," or "Names just fly right out of my head as soon as I hear them." They just make a point of getting good at remembering names, even writing them down if that helps.

They know how to start and keep a conversation going. They put good people together with each other, broadening everyone's network of positive connections.

Comfortable and confident, they lighten the mood when things are getting intense, and also manage to be in the right place when the best assignments and opportunities come up.

That's a long list, but there are people like this!

You may know some.

Beautiful someone, you're reading *Simply Irresistible* because you're becoming one!

Positive directions

Once we understand it and have solid strategies for boosting it every day, our own irresistibility earns us respect, makes us more effective at everything we try...and it does something even more important: it literally accelerates our success by strengthening our relationships and deepening our business connections with the people we work with and for.

As we build this amazing career asset, things begin to move in positive directions.

People confide in us, and that means we're in the loop — and in the know.

Since we have a reputation for being balanced and insightful, **people listen** to our opinions and ideas and take them seriously.

We're trusted with the **best assignments**.

We're invited into the room when **important decisions** are being made, increasing our influence.

But out of everything that an "irresistibility boost" lets us accomplish, its greatest power may be that it helps us be visible in positive ways.

Because whatever must-achieve career goal we're after:

- A new job

- More recognition

- A promotion or raise

- Better opportunities

- Sales

- Better team spirit

- Connecting with an influential person

...being irresistible has the power to put us in front of the right people and shortlisted for the best opportunities.

What's next then?

We get the job, promotion, or recognition we've earned.

People pay attention to our ideas and get behind them with real enthusiasm.

Good assignments and opportunities showcase our skills and potential.

Prospects become customers, and then raving fans.

We speak up with confidence and build a reputation as an expert.

Now look at us sitting there in the driver's seat of our own sweet awesome career!

@work!

The Blossie @work! series is a little different for us, beautiful someone, and I want to explain: I worked in the corporate world for a long time. And from that experience, I believe down to my bones that this moment, right now, is uniquely suited to bringing grace and kindness and gratitude and generosity and trust — all the ideas you and I share in Blossie's Books — to the world of work.

It's time to start seeing success at our jobs as something bigger than just money and power. And wherever they occur, this would be a great time to ditch productivity at the expense of creativity, winning by creating a loser, and competing rather than cooperating.

Sounds a little out there, maybe.

But wait...

For the longest time, I tried to fit in with companies and teams of people whose approach to their work was highly competitive, laser-focused on the "win" (whatever that meant in the moment), and unconcerned about the impact all this had on people — the actual *humans* who made the work happen in the first place. I'm not proud of it, but I really <u>did</u> try to fit in. Still, I just couldn't, and I guess that's the good news. Somehow my soul knew that "making it" as an employee in these kinds of workplaces wouldn't be a good thing.

"You need thicker skin" was something I heard at least once a week from well-meaning friends. My answer was always the same: "But I don't have a thick skin, and if I don't have one by now, maybe it's not happening?"

I'd leave work sometimes desperate to get home, change into a T-shirt and cargo pants, and run to the garden to dig in the dirt and feel healthy again.

I've learned a lot of things since then, but one of the most important is that work today has shifted. Workplaces, I think helped along by the salad bowl of work options for many people: online, offline, in-person and virtual, are changing into rare settings where we *can* have it both ways. We can enjoy work *and* succeed.

Our true lives (families, kitchens, basements, cars) are newly visible and accepted. Our in-person jobs in restaurants, gyms, grocery and retail stores can also get a lift from a new outlook of flexibility, kindness, respect, generosity, and support. I think all this progress, enabled by technology, has changed work permanently.

And in this new world of work, one in which we can be fully human and real, we can succeed and still be gracious and grateful and giving.

We can work, and instead of climbing over other people, we can take them with us.

And we can enjoy the work we do and the people we do it with and for.

As always, beautiful someone, I am hopeful.

Beginning

It's kind of poetic that I wrote the lion's share of *Simply Irresistible* crouched over a Chromebook at the back of the cafeteria in one of the worst jobs I ever had. The competition for credit was fierce, leading to idea-stealing and regular embarrassment over positive suggestions for change that were too often dismissed before they were even fully articulated.

My boss made people sweat and cry whenever possible and was a terrible gossip, usually unsupportive and occasionally downright cruel. People in my position came and went faster than the rest of us go through underwear.

The day I resigned, as I got ready for the inevitable conversation, I took a walk outside at lunch and heard just one word banging around in my head. *Intolerable.* Over and over again, just that word, *intolerable.* I knew I was making the right choice.

The good news is that was a new beginning because it was there, huddled in the back of that cafeteria, that I realized two things:

1) It didn't matter whether I had to work three jobs at once to feed my kids, I would never put myself in that kind of situation again, and

2) I knew what it was like to go to work every day twisted into knots, and I would never treat anyone working with

or for me in a remotely similar way. I would respect everyone enough to listen to their ideas, give them honest feedback, constructively and with kindness. I would listen with an inner ear to understand what they were experiencing and honor their struggles. I'd give them the support they needed to bloom and grow into the best they could be in their work lives.

My heart to yours, beautiful someone: may Blossie @work! turn this new beginning for me into ideas and strategies that help you too, first by changing the way you think about yourself at work and how you can treat people there. And then by slowly but surely changing the world of work around you.

Why us first?
We start by changing ourselves because grace and kindness often begin with changes we need to make to our *own* ways of thinking and working, to make ourselves more accepting, more gracious, and more generous at work. It makes sense that we can't give away what we don't have ourselves. But the reverse is also true: we can readily give away what we have in abundance.

My hope is that as we explore these Blossie @work! books together, we build the grace and the grit to be optimistic at work, to help others feel the same way, and to make every part of our lives, including (and in some ways, especially) work, happy, healthy, and sane.

This is the heart of Blossie @work! and an important theme running through *Simply Irresistible*.

So let's get started...
How do we know our irresistibility could use a boost?

Different ways.

We may sense that we're a little stuck in our jobs, and while we have some general ideas about why, we're not completely sure.

We feel like we're working below our potential. We're itching to move on and move up, maybe to a new situation or a new level...like a promotion, or a new job. Or we just feel a restlessness to do more.

We want to fill a new need, position, or opportunity with our talents.

We feel unrecognized for our work or our potential, no matter how hard we try to get noticed.

We may feel like we need to improve our listening or communication skills at work because we always seem to be out of the loop. What are we missing?

Maybe we've gotten the same feedback — the same confusion about our skills, experience, or goals — from people whose opinions matter to our future. We've never said or done anything to clear up the confusion, but we're starting to wish we had.

Beautiful someone, it's time to get rid of that feeling of restlessness, that sense that we could be doing more. Time to remember that great feeling of accomplishing something and going home. Exhaling, dropping our shoulders, closing the door on our work day, and then actually looking forward to the next one.

Time for an irresistibility boost.

The greatest secret: *give first*

No matter what job they have, irresistible people know how to do two things at work:

1) Tune into the needs of the people they work with and for, and

2) Generously give of their time, energy, and ideas.

In the process, they're positive, constructive, and encouraging, and they help out whenever they can, plus — this part's important — *they do all this expecting nothing in return.*

Then, the truly amazing thing: when they need something, all the people they've helped in the past show up and offer to help. Not every time and often not right away, but on the whole over time, that's exactly what happens. People knew they could rely on them, and those same people now want to return the favor.

This is just the greatest secret to receiving love and light, and, at work, to being simply irresistible:

If we want people to be interested in our opinions, we should hear theirs first.

If we want them to listen to our ideas, we should listen to theirs first.

If we want them to call us when the best opportunities come up, we should send a few their way first.

If we want them to connect us with an influential person, we should introduce them to a few of our favorite people first.

Let's get more specific.

Want them to promote us? We should make them look good whenever we can.

Give us a job? We should do some intense homework first and then talk to them about what we'll be able to do for them if we get the position.

Buy our product or service? We should offer them something of value at low or no cost first.

When we "give first" like this in our own work and lives, one day, we'll look around and see...

We're surrounded by people who think like us: coworkers, managers, mentors, and friends who are generous and genuinely caring.

Since we value their thinking and their positive, optimistic approach to work, they're our go-to people when we need a new idea or fresh solution...and we're theirs. They're having lunch with someone we've been thinking we'd like to meet. They're giving a presentation at the networking event we're attending. They're introducing us to influential people, making sure we're the first to know about exciting new opportunities, and telling us about resources that will help us.

Because we are high-impact, high-value people, we make our coworkers feel healthy and hopeful. They share their ideas with us, confident that we'll find even the smallest grain of positive potential and help them build on it.

Since we're on their minds so often, we're the ones they think of when a great assignment pops up. The ones they want to introduce to the influential decisionmaker. The person they can't help but help.

Pause for a second, beautiful someone and think about it: by giving first, this is the quality of people we attract into our circle of irresistible connections.

The best experiences, people, and opportunities start to show up for us, and the struggle to be noticed and respected loses its edge. Surrounded by positive energy and mutual support, we succeed, and maybe even better: we enjoy our work so much more.

Amazingly, by helping others win, we win.

By putting them first, we end up ahead.

Success is attracted to us in the form of amazing, positive, and equally generous people who show up for us the way we did for them. We are *simply irresistible*.

As a plus, we enjoy our work and the people we do it with so much more.

For these very reasons, the ideas and suggestions in *Simply Irresistible*, from putting people first to listening closely and encouraging them, are based on my heartfelt experience. I know that focusing on relationships, listening, sharing ideas, and other forms of generosity at work come back to us tenfold.

And once we understand this, we just need clear strategies to make it happen.

Under pressure
Smack in the middle of our hectic lives, it can feel really hard — sometimes just impossible — to focus on other people at work.

Our own needs, ideas, goals, and hopes seem to take all our energy. By the time we've dealt with our time pressures, money pressures, and work pressures (not to mention by the time we remember to register the kids for swim, buy milk on the way home, or find a plumber) there's not much of us left to focus on the needs of other people!

But, beautiful someone, as honest and understandable as this is, it's a slippery slope. When we give in to everyday work pressures by taking care of only our own needs, we can grow blinders and, unable to see anything outside our narrow view of the world, end up isolated. Before long, we're staring at a solid wall that's blocking us from the very people we need — the coworkers, mentors, important connections and influencers in our work lives, the people who help us get ahead with:

New contacts

Better information

Fresh ideas

New opportunities

"Okay, but what about..."

We all know people who do just the opposite and seem to get ahead anyway. They trample on coworkers or maybe they just don't seem to care what anyone thinks. No reason to go into detail about their behaviors; we all know what they are. Gossip. Hogging the spotlight. Bottomless self-concern.

But here's the thing: their MO may create success in the short term, but sooner or later, it catches up with them. They annoy the wrong person. They suddenly need help from someone they've hurt in the past. A new manager comes in who sees right through their "me-first" way of working. Long term, they end up alienated and isolated.

It's actually easy to find examples of people who worked this way, people who didn't see the light until it was too late. By the time they understood that their gains would be short term and only inside a small circle of people who were just as self-concerned and disloyal as they were, they'd lost opportunities and friends, in some cases permanently. Of the thousands of business people I've met, I have never known anyone who consistently put themselves first to be happy, healthy, or successful long term.

Seriously.

Real people

The VP who was hired in from another company and decided she wanted to bring in all her own people. She fired an entire team, including people who'd been there for years, with no concern for their situations, ideas, or hard work and dedication. She herself was let go within two years and ended up working as an Assistant Manager for a small car rental company.

The IT guy who hoarded information and technology insights to appear more knowledgeable than he rest of the team. He was found out for not forwarding a series of emails that could have prevented a serious hack which jeopardized huge amounts of data and hundreds of customer relationships. Gone that afternoon.

The line worker in a pharma plant who found a way to blame broken pills on just about everyone else. A new manager noticed her name on numerous quality control cases, raising a red flag. Unfortunately, because of her past behavior, no one raised a hand to vouch for her. She was reassigned to a less critical (and lower-paying) position.

This isn't just karma paying these people a visit. It's simple logic: they weren't trustworthy, so they couldn't trust anyone.

They were unkind, so they were surrounded by angry people.

They were disloyal, so people were hurt by them and then kept their distance.

Even without knowing the particulars of each of these stories, we can surmise the pattern: their actions hurt and frustrated people in their circle. Those people reacted by treating them the same way. They then reacted with more hurtful actions. These in turn led to more hurt...and so on in a downward spiral. The cynicism, self-concern, and eventually isolation they brought with them followed them out of every experience and every relationship they treated this way.

Irresistible people take the long view of relationships. They build them over time so these relationships can serve as the foundation for a lasting, prosperous, and fulfilling life and career, one with the staying power to help them make it through the tough times surrounded by people who believe in their goals, care about their success, and want to help them build it.

So here's the difference: having a long view of work relationships draws positive people and good experiences toward us. Plus, it's healthier and more fun, and it lets us enjoy our work and the people we do it with and for (Enjoy? Fun? Work, really? Yes!).

"Diana, you just don't know where I work..."

Anyone who's been in the workforce for more than a month knows how just how naïve all this sounds.

I get it, I do.

But two things: first, being naïve goes along with being hopeful. Hope looks beyond what is to what can be. What's possible. What we can create. And so right now, these ideas about positive workplaces and generous business relationships may sound naively blue-sky because maybe right now they are. But hope believes they can get better, more to the point: we can make them better.

Second, beautiful someone, change is always an inside-out proposition; it starts with the personal; it's us-first. And it's almost always gradual. So, we can believe in this hope-filled vision of the future ourselves (and be happier, healthier, and saner in the process). And we can find and create small changes in our immediate work circles and take them as signs of more good things to come.

Added benefit: we are the irresistible people at work who everyone is attracted to for our positive, hopeful attitude and sense of what's possible.

Beautiful someone, in *Simply Irresistible*, we're about to explore steps we can take to make ourselves irresistible to the best people, the best experiences, and the best opportunities.

Let's go!

I wish you blue skies and breakthroughs,

Diana

DIANA DAVIN

Put people first...

Give them your time

Show them they

matter

Irresistible people invest time in their work relationships. They surround themselves with hardworking and positive-thinking people. They know their success partners and invest in these critical relationships. They network like crazy, getting good people together and putting themselves in front of the right people at the right time.

DIANA DAVIN

Invest in relationships

"If you want to go fast, go alone.
If you want to go far, go together."

— Al Gore

We all know at least one super-successful person whose skills aren't top of the line.

We see the person's resume — experience, qualifications, skills — and think, "How did she ever become a General Manager with such average credentials?" But after getting to know the person, it's obvious: she succeeded by making people feel respected and valued.

She achieved by inspiring people with her ideas and infectious energy, both given out freely, without reservation or obligation. She clearly values people, and her work relationships mean as much to her as her own excellent performance in her job. In short, she succeeded by realizing that we can't go wrong, and in fact, we'll probably go very right, by putting people first in our career.

Not goals, not numbers, not recognition or promotions, but *people*.

Relationships are a high priority in the careers of irresistible people. Their work lives show a consistent investment of time and energy in relationship building, networking, and mentoring others. They know that no one succeeds alone, that every great achievement, turning point, promotion, plum assignment, and award they have received would not have been possible without the mentors who inspired them, the coworkers who gave them advice, the influential leaders who introduced them to key people, and the friends who cheered them on (or up 😊).

Irresistible people deliberately surround themselves with quality people: the highly successful, the influential, and the breakthrough bound. And just as important, they're skilled at avoiding negative people whose unhealthy energy, like a bad cold, can be incredibly infectious.

They keep their word in these important relationships. They show up for someone when they say they will, do what they said they would for people. If they hear something confidential, it stays confidential. *No exceptions.* And if workplace gossip is happening, irresistible people are nowhere to be found.

They know who their success partners are (the mentors, trusted coworkers, and key influencers in their work lives) and they ask them for help, using them as honesty springboards, accountability partners, and personal sages.

They also know that building relationships by networking, sharing contacts, and putting great people together is one of the most important and high-impact applications of creating irresistible relationships. By taking the initiative to create opportunities for others to connect and complement each other's skills or just share great ideas with each other, irresistible people generate vibrant energy that flows from them through these connections and back again.

Jack's story — not helpless
When the economy plummeted, countless small businesses folded. Jack, the owner of an alarm installation company with 17 employees, watched and held his breath, feeling helpless. Customers stopped calling, jobs disappeared. He went to bed and

woke up in the same agitated frame of mind. "It was like having a brick sitting on my chest all the time," he said. "Some of my employees had young families and new mortgages. One had a wife who was very ill, and I was in a panic about our medical plan."

Then one day, he ran into a building manager he knew. Years earlier, Jack had helped this person get the job he now had. "I think I know a few people you can call," the man told him. That got Jack thinking: "Who else have I helped in the past?" He planned a few things to say, then picked up the phone and started calling people he knew, especially the ones he'd helped with business or bargains.

"That was the greatest lesson I ever got about business," Jack said. "My relationships saved my company and protected my family and my employees. I kept all my employees with me and made not one change to their medical coverage," he explained with genuine relief in his voice.

"I think a lot of times we say relationships are important in business," he concluded, "but I don't think I knew just how important until then. Long term, the favors you do for people all come back to help you – times ten."

Sara's story – the connection queen

Sara lost her job as Communications Manager at an insurance company in the worst job market in decades.

Sara had a strong network of contacts in her old company and in her industry, people she'd helped over the years. "That was always such a natural part of my personality," she said, "I like being helpful, so I would always connect people to each other and get jobs for friends who needed them. It was just something I did.

"I also get excited when I hear about an opportunity and then can think of someone who would be a great fit for it," she continued. "To me, it's like putting the pieces of a puzzle together — who do I know for this assignment? Who'd be great in this job? Who should this person know? I'd connect buyers and vendors, people looking for help with projects, and always people looking for work with new job openings."

When Sara lost her job, all the people she'd helped — their "connection queen" they called her — showed up to help.

"What was amazing," she said, "was that I had more interviews than I could handle that first month, and I had a job offer in six weeks!"

She concluded, "It was a humbling experience, and one I'll never forget. You always remember the lessons you learn when you're at your lowest point."

Beautiful someone, if we want to be top of mind when someone is looking to fill a critical role on a high visibility project or award a unique opportunity that matches our skillset, we need to follow the lead of irresistible people like Jack and Sara by making relationships top priority.

Let's go...

Irresistible relationship-building

Humans @ work

Ever run into a coworker outside of work and been shocked to see the person with a spouse or significant other whom you've never met, dressed down, unshaven, or without makeup? Or watched someone interact with their family at a company event and been shocked to realize how "regular" they seem? How just like you?

Everyone — every single person we work with — is a human being with a home, a family, friends, hobbies, maybe a pet or two. They have to pay bills, buy milk, and wash dishes. When we see them only at work every day, we tend to forget this. We know them in only one small way, one tiny slice of the total human being who's walking, talking, breathing, eating lunch...working! next to us.

Think about how much easier it would be to deal with that difficult coworker or manager if we remembered this. When conflict arises, when someone is less than cordial, when they make a careless mistake — imagine if we could look past the problem, just package it up and put it aside for a minute, and see the individual, the regular person just like us.

The problem we may be having with them hasn't disappeared — they still didn't invite us to the meeting, they criticized our presentation, they didn't email the information we needed — but it's simpler somehow. It's just the issue, all by itself, perpetrated by a regular imperfect human, just like us. We can see it for just what it is, and that makes it easier to be objective about it and handle it powerfully. We can simply ask ourselves what we can do next time to be sure this human being invites us to the meeting or sends the information we need.

Here's the real point: how much more powerful would we feel? How much more prepared to tackle the obstacle, while keeping the relationship strong? How much more appealing would we be to other professionals looking for a steady, unemotional approach to inevitable conflicts and difficulties?

And in the final analysis, how much more *irresistible* would we be?

What's in a name? (A lot!)

One of the most beautiful sounds anyone can hear is the sound of their own name. This is why irresistible people don't allow themselves to say, "Oh, I'm terrible with names!" They just make a point of memorizing names, and they do it consistently.

So when you meet someone, no matter what it takes, *remember their name.* Text it to yourself. Write it down. Repeat it a few times silently with a visual cue or reminder. "Janet, Janet. She reminds me of a girl named Jane I grew up with. That fits her to a T. Jane-t."

Then use it a few times looking directly at the person to anchor the name in your mind to the image of the face:

- "Hi Janet! Great to meet you."

- "The one thing I want to be really clear on Janet is whether you think..."

- "Janet, thanks so much for letting me know."

Good vibes

"How are you doing?"

"What's new?"

"What are you working on?"

"What's happening with you?"

With just a few words like these, irresistible people show genuine interest in the people they work with and for, sending them a clear message: "You're important to me." Right away, the person on the receiving end of these good vibes knows two things: 1) the person talking sincerely cares about them, and 2) there's a good chance they'll help them out, whatever they need.

There's something subtle going on here too: when we value someone's interests and concerns, we value *them*. And we can be sure that supportive vibe is coming across to them as loud and clear as if we were yelling, "I care about you! I respect you!" through a megaphone.

Take a look at this real exchange between two coworkers:

"Marc, can you look at these figures and let me know if they're accurate? I need them back ASAP."

"You mean next year's budget? How did the planning go? Couldn't have been fun this year."

"Yeah, true story. Frustrating. Too many cuts and too much to do with too little money."

"Right. That's really hard, especially right now."

"Definitely. So can I count on you to get this done for me today?"

"Today's really busy, but I know this is important. I have a deadline this afternoon, but I can take a quick look after it's done and then again in the morning when I'm fresh. Can you talk tomorrow at 10?"

"Perfect, thanks."

And this one:

"Hi Jo. I need to talk to you."

"Okay sure. How are you doing by the way? I know you guys have been working 24/7 on that filing."

"Actually, I am exhausted, and Gabe asked me to help you with your presentation to the Management Committee next week."

"I would actually love your help. But let's work it out so you can get some sleep first! How about later this week? I'll get started in the meantime and when we get together, I can show you what I have."

"That would be great. Thanks for the extra time."

"You got it."

The honest concern Marc and Jo are showing in these conversations is so clear. As they show how much they appreciate the other person's priorities and the pressures they're under and then offer to help, even in a small way, they send out a kind of empathetic professional energy.

And what's important is what's being said, but also what isn't.

Take a look now at the statements in italics, the subtle messages being conveyed:

"Marc, can you look at these figures and let me know if they're accurate? I need them back this afternoon."

"You mean next year's budget? How did the planning go? That's usually a tough process." *[I understand what you're going through.]*

"True story. Frustrating. Too many cuts and too much to do with too little money."

"Right. That's really hard, especially right now." *[I know that you're in a tough spot and you want to get this right.]*

"Definitely. So can I count on you to get this done for me today?"

"Today's really busy, but I know this is important. I have a deadline this afternoon, but I can take a quick look after it's done and then again in the morning when I'm fresh. Can you talk tomorrow at 10?" *[I really want to help you. Here's a way I can do it that's a win for both of us.]*

"Perfect, thanks."

Here's the second one:

"Hi Jo. I need to talk to you."

"Okay sure. How are you doing by the way? I know you guys have been working 24/7 on that filing." *[I know what you're going through. I'm concerned about you.]*

"Actually, I am exhausted, and Gabe told me to help you with your presentation to the Management Committee next week."

"I would actually love your help. But let's work it out so you can get some sleep first! How about later this week? I'll get started in the meantime and when we get together, I can show you what I have." *[I respect your expertise and need your help, and I want to be sure you know how grateful I am that you're doing me a favor. I can use your time better if I work on this first so when we sit down, there's something to look at.]*

"That would be great. Thanks for the extra time."

"You got it."

Here's the amazing thing: the people Marc and Jo are talking to will hear the spoken words with their ears, but what will shout loud and clear to them will be what's in italic. It's also what they'll remember, long after they forget the specifics of the situation.

As Nobel Prize winning poet Maya Angelou said, "People will forget what you did, but they will never forget how you made them feel."

Equal chances

Have you ever started a new position and had someone say to you, "Be careful of Rachel. She's so hard to work with," or "Steer clear of Ben. He takes the credit for everything"?

Before you've even met either of these people, a negative opinion has started to take shape in your mind. Apart from not giving Rachel or Ben a fair chance — maybe Rachel has changed. And what if the negative experience wasn't all Ben's fault? When you do finally work with these people, these opinions (and they are just opinions) are negative filters in your mind that Rachel and Ben's words and actions have to pass through before they get to you.

In reality though, these opinions are based on *someone else's* experiences. And who knows? Maybe Rachel is actually easy to work with, while the person sharing their opinion with you isn't. Ben may take all the credit, but it's possible he tends to work harder than anyone else and actually deserves more of the credit!

Plus, the dynamic between people can be as unique as a fingerprint. You may actually click with Rachel where others don't, but until you work with her yourself, you won't know. Ben may be excited to collaborate with you because you inspire higher levels of trust from him than anyone else.

Bottom line: irresistible people <u>never</u> let someone else's experiences shape their opinions and their relationships.

Let's follow their example, never running our unique and precious lives and careers based on the experiences and opinions (especially negative ones) of other people. We can give everyone an equal chance to earn our professional trust and respect, never ever looking at people through the prism of anyone else's experiences or opinions.

Let's respect ourselves enough, beautiful someone, to create our own.

Success partners

Think about the greatest achievements of your work life. The promotion, the plum assignment, the award, the new account or client you won.

Isn't it amazing how memory travels back not only to what happened, but who was there — who inspired you, gave you advice and encouragement, introduced you to a key person, helped promote your skills to a decision maker, or just cheered you on? We remember these people so clearly because their support and encouragement helped make the achievement possible. They were there when we really needed them.

In his book *Relationships 101*, leadership expert and best-selling author John Maxwell says that, "Becoming a highly relational person brings individual and team success." By "highly relational" Maxwell is referring to the skill of building relationships with a healthy give-and-take of advice, information, and support.

No one can succeed alone, and if we look at the careers of ultra-successful people, we see a pattern of relationship building, long-term alliances, strong work friendships and a reliance on colleagues and networks. Irresistible people know that their work relationships are as important to their success as their own brains and heart.

Each type of work relationship is unique, though they have one common characteristic: they are based on trust and honesty.

Trusted coworkers

These are work friends, usually peers, we trust completely and can easily talk to.

Examples:

Current and former coworkers

Friends who work in similar jobs or industries

Networking connections

Work friends we met through a vendor or workshop

Trusted coworkers always have our backs. They give us objective, realistic feedback keeping our best interests at heart. They're honest sounding boards who are kind but don't put lots of window dressing on their feedback.

These people broaden our perspective with input and insights we're not capable of on our own. They'll let us vent to them and they'll tell us the truth. We can't survive without them.

Next up: mentors

Mentors are people whose success we admire and would like to emulate. Mentors are role models whose support and advice prevent us from having to "reinvent the wheel" and save us from making the mistakes they made. Mentors are usually a level or two above us in rank or achievement; they've earned a measure of success beyond ours. When handled well, a mentor relationship can be a career-long asset.

Examples:

A company leader or manager

A fellow business owner

A boss or former boss

A successful person in our profession or industry

A third group is key influencers

These are our gatekeepers. The people in our work lives whose opinions of our performance and potential have the greatest impact on our progression, growth, and success. Influencers can open doors for us, introducing us to key people, spotlighting our skills or accomplishments at key moments, or pulling strings to send plum assignments or opportunities our way.

Examples:

People senior to us where we work (our own manager/leader or the people they work with and for)

Influential peers in the company

If we own a business...
— All our connection sources: our largest clients and best customers
— Fellow members in professional organizations who have benefited from our products or services
— Vendors we partner with to serve our customers or clients

Identify three to five individuals in each category and nurture these important relationships through ongoing contact and communication.

Take good care of these relationships and they'll take care of you!

A little slack

"I would *never* allow..."

"She shouldn't have..."

"I wasn't there, but he was totally wrong."

"They're never going to make the deadline. They miss every one!"

"He did an awful job with that meeting. He just threw it together because he doesn't even care."

Not really (☺). Unless someone is in the absolutely identical position, with every fact and circumstance a literal carbon copy of what the person they're judging is going through (job pressures, career goals, work history, family life, and literally everything else...), there's no way to know the absolute right thing to do.

Much better for irresistible relationship-building: giving the person the benefit of the doubt. (I know. I know. It's so hard sometimes! Still...) Assume they made a mistake, had the best intentions, that they're under pressure, stressed about a deadline, just not thinking clearly. Graciously accept their off-putting, annoying, or maddening actions without expecting anything, not even a "Thank you" in return.

Sounds like we're letting them get away something, right? Yeah, we probably are. But, BUT...almost always, giving someone the benefit of the doubt does more for us than it does for them.

Think of it: so we sacrifice the momentary relief of a gut-level reaction, from visible annoyance all the way to outright accusation. In return, we get so much: less stress. Fewer arguments. Much less negativity. More coworkers trusting us. More energy left for the good stuff (our goals, connections, promotions, projects, futures).

No need to waste our professional energy on anger, dueling egos, and senseless debates over low-impact issues. We're not constantly at war with coworkers, thinking about where things stand, who's winning and who's on our side. We don't have to anticipate our opponent's countermoves and just generally work in stress and strife...all of which just drains the life out of us.

An easygoing, "I'm going to give Ali a pass on this one" saves our passions for better things. It also increases the likelihood that Ali will do the same for us when we need it.

What a relief!

As a plus, giving someone the benefit of the doubt calms us down. As we try to imagine what the person may be going through or what the situation looks like through their eyes, we begin to see the human being rather than the perpetrator of the exasperating behavior. Our anger cools. We relax.

It *does* take emotional strength to assume that the person didn't mean to be rude or that they're having a bad day or made an honest mistake and then react with a light attitude:

"I understand...I've had bad days too!"

"He probably meant to spend more time planning the meeting but it just crept up on him."

"It looks like they're really struggling with that deadline. Let me see if I can help."

"She did what she did. I can't judge that. I wasn't there."

...but what an amazing payoff!

As we discipline our thoughts and control our reactions, we also feel a surge of personal power and self-control. When we give someone slack without concern for what we may lose or receive in return, we're not vulnerable to disappointment. Because we expect nothing back, we can't be hurt or insulted if it doesn't come. Cynicism, bitterness, and resentment may search for a foothold in our work life beautiful someone, but they won't find one.

If we still need more reasons to consider this power-packed approach to irresistibility, we can just think back to a time when we desperately wanted someone to look the other way or to just forget a stupid mistake we made. And remember how, when they did, we were filled with gratitude, the kind that made us see that person differently for a long time to come, maybe even permanently. Remember how much we appreciated their understanding at that low point in our career when we felt exposed and vulnerable, when we wanted nothing more than to forget it and for everyone else to do the same?

The goodwill that irresistible person extended to us earned them our gratitude, friendship, and loyalty probably for years to come.

Now, we can be that person!

Return favors...plus!

Lots of people express gratitude for the help they receive. They say "Thanks," and maybe make a mental note to return the favor if they can.

Irresistible people do that and more — they go above and beyond to show their sincere gratitude for any help they get. They take the time to publicly recognize people for even the smallest act of support or words of encouragement, acknowledging out loud what's been done for them. In the process, they showcase someone else as a talented contributor and share the credit for achievements that were made possible by someone's help, information, or support

And their gratitude is active in other ways. They turn thanks into a verb, energetically looking for ways to help a coworker who's helped them. There is a constant flow of generous words and actions sent out from them in the direction of anyone who helps them in even the smallest way.

Let's remember the people who help us out and actively look for ways to return the favor:

> "Thanks for inviting me to the meeting, Kate. To follow up, I wanted to send you this article I thought you'd find interesting."

> "I appreciate the cc, Sierra. Good to be looped in! Please let me know if there are any projects I'm working on that you'd like to be involved in."

> "Keon, here's Jo's number. I've cc'd her on this note because I think she could benefit from the great sales data you shared with me yesterday. And thanks again, by the way!"

> "Celine, I want you to meet the people I know on the Finance team. They are outsourcing experts who could help HR with what you're working on."

> "Drew, thanks for your help yesterday! Are you free for lunch…it's on me. Would be great to hear about what else you're working on because I'd like to return the favor."

Knowledge sharing

We all know, "Knowledge is power." The more we know, the stronger we are. The more intelligent decisions we can make.

The more feasible and pragmatic our ideas can be. The more worthwhile our feedback. The sharper our questions.

These are just a few of the reasons that in business, knowledge is such a valuable commodity.

So it's natural that sometimes, we're tempted to keep breakthrough news and important ideas to ourselves. If we keep control over this knowledge, it feels like we keep the power too.

Irresistible people do their best not to give in to this temptation! They know that while knowledge is power, that same knowledge in the hands of a supportive, collaborative team of people who genuinely care about each other is much more powerful. They understand that rather than diminish their own influence, sharing information multiplies it — exponentially, building incredibly strong relationships in the process.

The habit of knowledge sharing — which starts with the mental and emotional discipline to ask, "Who else should know about this?" every day — also sends a clear message that we're thinking about people, have a generous spirit and believe in the power of people working in concert toward goals they want to reach.

The result is more complete ideas, deeper insights, and broader thinking...and of course, irresistible work relationships.

Here's how we can do the same...

Look for ways to help people with information you come across. Forward articles, sites, and experts' contact information to them.

When you learn or experience something new, make a habit of thinking about who else could benefit from knowing about it.

— If you attend a workshop for instance, can send coworkers links to the handouts and other resources.

— If you go to a networking meeting, forward contact information from the interesting people you meet to coworkers, maybe even making introductions.

Then, watch as the power of information and access multiplies exponentially for the benefit of everyone, and quickly comes back to you with irresistible energy – ten times over!

Put good people together

"The whole is greater than the sum of its parts," wrote Aristotle in the first century. And it's true...at work, we can't calculate the total power of a group just by adding up the contributions of individual members, one by one. The reason is that when two or more people come together, a third entity is created – the group – with a unique combination of intelligence and abilities and exponential energy.

Irresistible people know this. They attract the best people and experiences. Then they take the next step: they help create brand new alliances by putting these people together with each other. Seeing great people meeting each other for the first time and then working together to solve a problem or create something new is a great thrill for them. They are constantly on the lookout for opportunities to put people with complementary needs and skills together with each other.

Here's what this sounds like:

"Jon, let me introduce you to someone I think you'd really enjoy meeting."

"Sara, I want to connect you with an expert in this area, who also happens to be one of my favorite people."

This is such a classy (and irresistible) way to operate!

So let's do this...think of people you know who would work together well, people whose skills and needs are naturally drawn together: salespeople and marketers, researchers and designers, trainers and communicators, and definitely recruiters and job seekers.

We may hesitate to make these kinds of connections and introduce people to each other out of fear that things might not go well, and we don't want our reputation tarnished if they don't. Let's take the pressure off ourselves! We're just giving the connection a jumpstart when we put good people together; we're just making the introduction. Then, we can step back! The people involved need to make it work from there.

So make the introduction, and step away. Most of the time, these synergistic relationships will work out well. And, in a nod to true irresistibility, we can be sure the people we've connected to one another will one day return the favor!

Ask an expert (or be one!)

What could we accomplish at work if we had easy and regular access to experts of all kinds? If a phone call or email could connect us with someone willing and able to help us with great advice and information?

Irresistible people know. They understand the value of deliberately surrounding themselves with experts they can turn to for career development ideas or solid advice on a tough situation, high-impact issue, problem, challenge, or opportunity. They know exactly where to find people who will point them in the direction of resources and ideas that will enable them to jump the learning curve and reach their goals faster.

Rather than struggle for a week trying to solve a problem on their own, they ask an expert. They find someone who knows about new tools and methods for working smarter and getting more done in less time. Someone familiar with that new software they'd like to use. Someone who's read the books, done the research, published the posts.

The irresistible habit of seeking out experts does more than save time. It forges new relationships with experienced people on positive terms (everyone loves to be recognized as an expert and asked for advice!).

Irresistible people also look for opportunities to *be* the expert when someone else needs advice on a topic they know well. They enjoy the one-of-a-kind satisfaction that comes from helping others succeed. Many irresistible people will say that this satisfaction alone makes them feel like sharing their expertise gains them much more than they give.

But there's more, because in the process of helping others, irresistible people build awareness of their own knowledge and expertise, strengthen breakthrough skills like their ability to instruct, guide, and develop people and build their reputation for volunteerism, leadership, teamwork, and collaboration.

So, how can we actively and energetically look for opportunities to be the expert in a situation...

Who can we help?

Who needs our one-of-a-kind expertise or knowledge?

Who can we mentor?

Where can we volunteer?

Something to build on
"Let me give you some constructive criticism..."

Uh oh. Time to look for the exits.

Because we're probably about the get some feedback that's more critical than it is constructive. As it zeros-in on what's missing and what's wrong, most "constructive criticism" breaks down more than it builds, leaving the listener defensive and closed off, sometimes embarrassed too. If they leave their ears open long enough to actually hear any of it, they just end up uncomfortable and not at all motivated to try again. In this way, criticism of any kind never strengthens relationships. Instead, it splinters them.

Dale Carnegie devoted an entire chapter of his most well-known book, *How to Win Friends and Influence People* to the topic of criticism. He titled the chapter, "If You Want to Gather Honey, Don't Kick Over the Beehive." In it, he illustrated one of his core principles: "Don't criticize, condemn, or complain."

After taking readers through stories about the impact of criticism on the lives of everyone from notorious criminals to statesmen like Benjamin Franklin and Abraham Lincoln, Carnegie pulled no punches when he advised:

> If you and I want to stir up a resentment tomorrow that may rankle across the decades and endure until death, just let us indulge in a little stinging criticism — no matter how certain we are that it is justified...Anyone can criticize, condemn and complain...it takes character and self-control to be understanding and forgiving.

Out of the thousands of people I've worked with, I have yet to meet anyone who truly appreciates criticism. Think about it: when someone says, "Let me offer you some constructive criticism: never start a project like this before talking to someone from the department," or, "I have to be honest with you, this really missed the mark." We wither and droop, and our whole focus is on the mistakes they believe we made, which, in the spirit of "constructive criticism," they are likely to point out in exhaustive detail.

Criticism almost always produces one reaction: defensiveness. Defensive people aren't listening. They can't listen because the criticism has closed off the flow of ideas as surely as if we were turning a faucet hard right.

On the other hand, when someone starts their feedback with a comment that's truly constructive, like, "This looks good. I like where you're headed," or "Thanks for getting this done so fast," or "I like the way you handled the situation with Chris," we feel appreciated, encouraged, and open to whatever might be coming next.

And this way of giving someone feedback is effective whether the work is excellent or frankly, not so excellent. Either way, starting with positives and encouraging someone to build on them provides a hopeful context that opens the person's mind to constructive ideas for making their work better, their idea more workable, their resume stronger.

Balanced and positive
Irresistible people are masters at offering truly constructive feedback that's positive, balanced and motivating. They consistently check their integrity by offering suggestions that help others grow in some way. Their feedback gives the recipient ideas to build on. It leads with strengths and positives, and then

offers suggestions for improvement using those strengths, like this:

"Your [*work/idea/result*] is already good, and because I believe in you, I know you can make it even better."

They always provide suggestions for improvement the person can use next time, for instance:

"You might want to try..."

or

"Something I've done in those situations that's helpful is..."

When they offer suggestions, they are as specific as possible:

"I really liked the way you handled that situation, particularly when you said..."

"The second half of that project must have been really tough to sell to the team. How did you manage to get everyone to agree to the approach?"

Then, they offer clear, honest ideas in the spirit of helping the person go from "good" to "better," rather than from "awful" to "acceptable."

More real-work examples of how they offer this quality of feedback:

"I know project management is a strength of yours, Jose. You were the one who kept us focused last month so we didn't veer off course on the purchasing initiative. What did you do in that situation that you can apply here?"

"The second half of last year's procurement project was tough to sell to the team, but you managed to pull everyone together and get full agreement. What team/consensus-building skills did you use on that project? How can they be applied here?"

"Hey, you pushed us through that IT/Customer Service conflict last month. You can definitely handle this. Remember how you insisted that IT/Customer Service meet in the middle? What's the win in this situation for each side? How can you frame it for these two employees so it's clear they each stand to gain something by getting along?"

This is constructive feedback, and it's so much easier to hear, which means it's more likely *to* be heard, taken to heart, and turned into productive action.

Constructive feedback is fertile ground for progress at work...both for the person we're providing it to and for our relationship with them. It shows respect, confidence in them, and belief that they have the power to create an even better future. That makes truly constructive feedback both irresistible and self-fulfilling: we get a better quality of work because the person understands that we have faith in their abilities, and in them.

And BTW, the need for constructive feedback applies to everyone, even the most experienced people and even people who act like they don't need compliments, like Josh, Government Affairs Liaison for an aerospace company, who admitted, "I'd never say this at work because I think it makes me look weak, but I feel so motivated when the person I report to says I'm going a good job. It makes me willing to run through a wall for that person."

That makes truly constructive feedback one irresistible way of operating!

Good graces

Good graces, essentially carefully chosen words and actions that show respect and consideration for coworkers' time, feelings, and needs, are sometimes laughed off as quaint and old-fashioned: "No one cares about that stuff anymore!" or "Who has time to worry about being polite when we're under so much pressure every day?"

Irresistible people do. In fact, they *make* the time. Good graces make work more welcoming for everyone, and they create a climate of mutual respect and understanding that are powerful relationship-building tools.

I did a quick survey of friends, people I consider irresistible, in all types of jobs, from teachers to health care workers to corporate employees. Just one question: "What are the good graces you think are important at work?"

Here are some of their best (most irresistible!) ideas:

- "Know how to pronounce everyone's name. Especially today when we have business contacts from all over the world, it's a sign of respect to know how to say a person's name correctly."

- "Don't do 12 other things while I'm talking to you! Don't take calls or return texts or look over my shoulder at everyone walking by. And don't put me on speaker and then do other things while we're talking. First of all, *I can hear you!* Second, it makes me think that literally anything else is more interesting than what I'm saying."

- "Compliment people in ways that make them feel valued for what they do. Call a designer's slides 'genius.' Tell your office manager he's amazing at organizing everything. Publicly thank your marketing assistant for being

47

an ace at sticking to the production schedule on a project."

- "Be on time for calls and meetings and cancel only if you absolutely have to. Everyone is busy, and lateness sug-gests we think we're more important than the people we're inconveniencing."

- "Reread your emails before you send them to be sure they make sense and answer the questions someone's asked you. Write so it's easy on the reader...not on you!"

- "Keep your word...do what you say you're going to do. Period."

- "Listen to people's ideas, even if you think they won't work. You can be wrong, you know!"

- "Don't gossip! When you don't gossip, no one will gossip about you."

Change history (sort of)

Remember the game of telephone? One person would whisper something in someone's ear who'd whisper it to the next person and so on down the line. As the message passed from person to person, it got distorted. By the time the last person in line would say it out loud, it would sound nothing like the original.

Memory can work this way too. We sometimes distort and exaggerate old conflicts. We add a line here, a feeling there, and the story picks up more (sometimes a lot more) negative emotional content than it had at first, a sharper edge, greater embarrassment, more pain.

We may not realize it, but by adding emotional weight to it, we're making a conflict or any negative experience more significant, harming our relationships by treating them as defining moments that determine how we see other people and our relationships with them. Any time there's a chance to break new ground, there's that old conflict again from two years ago, and the thought looms, "I'd try, except I remember that time when I worked with him..."

But we can also do the opposite. After all, at this point, it's just a story we're recalling from memory, right? We can't change the event, but we can absolutely change how we think and talk about the event. Instead of maximizing its negative emotional impact, we can minimize it, and preserve the relationship in the process.

So rather than say, "That vendor ripped me off and then lied about it to my face!" we can say, "There was a serious miscommunication, including some dishonesty, which I now know how to avoid."

Instead of calling a bad situation "a total disaster," we can say, "Things didn't go as planned, but now I plan every detail."

"I won't be bossed around by my feelings"

Take any relationship book off the shelf, open a page, and there's a good chance you'll see some form of encouragement to get your feelings out in the open. "Talk it out!" they say. "Share your feelings!" That sounds sensible when you're talking about a friendship or a romance, where honesty and sharing matter for intimacy and connection, but these ideas don't exactly work in business. It's just not appropriate to sit down for a heart-to-heart with a coworker who's been making your life miserable and talk about how he's made you feel.

When conflict blindsides us at work, someone hits a hot button, criticizes us, takes credit for our work, ignores our emails, deliberately excludes us, or dismisses our ideas, surprise stops us in our tracks. Or maybe, on a day already chock full of pressure, a conflict that's been brewing for months rears its head, and we've finally had enough.

Adrenaline pumping, heart racing, hands sweating, the temptation to let it rip is almost irresistible, and we have a 100 percent organic reaction, spoken or silent:

- "No, you're wrong!"

- "Well, that was rude."

- "That's it! I've had enough of this!"

- "Stop accusing my team of ..."

- "Hey, that was a nasty thing to do."

- "Oh give me a break! That's completely untrue!"

- "That's totally unfair!"

Whether we lash out or hold our peace, anger is at the controls. That racing heart, the sweaty hands? They are preparing us for battle. Physiologically, anger triggers the "fight or flight" response hardwired into us by thousands of years of conditioning.

To spice things up a bit, this part of the brain is triggered so quickly that the prefrontal cortex, that blessed part of our minds responsible for reflection, good judgment, and decision making, doesn't have time to do its job.

Muscles (and voices) are ready before wisdom kicks in.

Since our minds don't distinguish a real, physical threat from a perceived or nonphysical one, the biological reaction is the same, whether we're looking at a charging grizzly or an email critical of our work.

This is the time to put relationships first and realize two things: a) we need to take a break, and b) the few moments of relief we feel after saying what's really on our minds in these situations are not worth the relationship-harming mess we'll have to clean up afterward.

Mess? Oh definitely. Because at work, letting it rip is costly, not just to the immediate relationship, but to every relationship that emanates from it. Essentially, we don't know who knows who at work.

After a single fallout, it's tough to know just how many bridges we've burned. One thing is sure: it's never just one. Author and master salesman Joe Girard created "Girard's Law of 250" which says that every person knows about 250 other people. That means burning one bridge burns *250 more*! So we lose not just one relationship, but access to every relationship that person has, his entire network of contacts and friends. We also end up looking over our shoulder for a long time, thinking, "I wonder if Drew knows Lee."

Be ultra-careful about burning bridges in this very small (and increasingly interconnected) work world.

Starting now, catch yourself when you react emotionally to a work conflict. Stop. Take a breath. Decide then and there that relationship-harming anger, frustration, fear, or disappointment will not run your career and reputation. *You* will. Think about your goals, the importance of the relationship, and what's truly at stake. Then, instead of reacting on pure emotion, make conscious choices to take command of yourself and the situation.

As always, beautiful someone, we have a choice to make, and we can choose composure, grace, professionalism...the high ground.

It's where irresistible people meet.

See you there!

*To effectively communicate,
we must realize that we are all different
in the way we perceive the world
and use this understanding as a
guide to our communication with others.*

— Anthony Robbins

Listen so people will talk...

Hear their ideas
Know their stories

Irresistible people have a clear awareness of what's happening in a situation, what matters to and motivates the people around them, and how to create wins for every-one involved.

That all starts with listening.

In the loop...and in the know

> "Listening is a magnetic and
> strange thing — a creative force.
> The friends who listen to us
> are the ones we move toward."
>
> — Karl Menniger

Is there anything better than knowing — not just believing, but knowing in your bones — that someone is truly listening to you, that they're "getting it"? The person values your ideas and dreams and *you*. Just by truly listening to you, they're making a real effort to get to know you.

After working with thousands of people facing work challenges large and small, honestly no communication skill has stood out as more career- and irresistibility-boosting than the ability to listen.

This is because listening at work does a lot more than help us gather information.

It shows we pay attention to detail.

It demonstrates our genuine concern for the issues that affect other people.

It shows our honest desire to get a job done right.

Most important, it shows we have a sincere interest in what matters to the people who matter to us.

Regardless of the situation, listening opens hearts, minds, and doors of opportunity. And it has another superpower: when people know we're listening — when they feel heard and supported — they sense that they're respected. Taking the time to listen sends a clear message: "I'm giving you my full attention because I value what you have to say."

Then the real magic begins: they relax and open up, and so we learn more and gather the information we need. Importantly, when we hear people, they're genuinely willing to hear us too. So later when it's our turn to talk, they listen to us. They feel a connection to us because just by listening, we built a bridge to them that they'll willingly cross over to meet us. A foundation of trust has taken hold.

It makes complete sense then...

If we want to connect with someone, we've got to listen first so we know what they value and how we can help provide it.

If we want to get a job or promotion, we've got to listen carefully so we know what our audience needs and how our qualifications are the perfect fit.

If we want to persuade someone, we need to listen so we understand their point of view before we can help them agree with ours.

Listening is basic equipment for irresistible people and a critical work skill we can all strengthen.

Let's start there...

Irresistible listening

Make the time

"I have to leave at 3."

"But it's 2:45, and you just got here."

"I know, plus Zack and the kids are waiting for me in the car."

"But I thought we were going to spend some time together."

"We are! I've got about ten minutes. I think I'll have a latte. So, tell me: why the tears?"

Regardless of what we want to accomplish, whether it's to get a new job, a promotion, more opportunity, a new sale or anything else, listening is powerful. But here's the thing: it's impossible to really listen in a hurry.

So our first irresistibility-boosting idea is to make time to listen. Forge a genuine connection to someone by setting aside time for an important conversation with them. We can literally put them on our schedule with a date, time, and place. Then, keep the time dedicated: no appointments right before or after that squeeze it out, leaving just minutes for the actual conversation (during which time we'll probably end up watching the clock instead of listening anyway).

If an important conversation comes up unexpectedly, we can turn off whatever we're doing – put the phone down especially — so we can listen completely, and if this isn't possible, we can ask to schedule the conversation: "This sounds important, but I'm working on something right now and want to give you my full attention. Are you free today at 2 to talk about it?"

Or, "This is too important to rush. Can we schedule time so I can really focus? Do you have time tomorrow morning?"

When we set aside the time like this, the other person hears us saying, loud and clear: "This conversation matters to me, *because you do.*"

Irresistible!

Listen. Just listen.

Have you ever tried to talk to someone at work who keeps peeking at their phone? How about a coworker who forgets the details of a conversation you *just* had with them or someone you just met who can't remember your name literally one minute later?

How about someone whose eyes are constantly darting around the room while you're talking? Or a coworker who makes you feel rushed all the time, like no matter how fast you talk, it's not fast enough? Or someone who always manages to shift the conversation toward themselves, no matter what the topic?

I have!

And I remember how uncomfortable and even unimportant these experiences made me feel. It wasn't just that they weren't listening. It was that anything and everything else seemed to be more interesting than what I had to say. And that if I stopped talking mid-sentence, they wouldn't even notice!

As bestselling author M. Scott Peck wrote, "You can't truly listen to anyone and do anything else at the same time." It doesn't matter if we can listen to someone, check email, and read an article at the same time.

What <u>does</u> matter is the message our actions are sending to the person who's talking — and how we're making them feel. That's what they'll remember, long after the specific topic fades from memory.

So let's make a simple commitment: when someone is talking, let's put everything on hold and tell ourselves, "Right now, I'm listening, and that's all I'm doing."

Look directly at the speaker. No matter who walks by, resist the urge to look over their shoulder. Don't allow your eyes to dart toward your laptop, phone, or anything you have to do. These distracting habits interrupt the person's thoughts as they stop to wonder what's more important or interesting than what they're talking about.

It's definitely not easy to ignore the umpteen distractions pulling at us: the calls, texts, emails, alerts, headlines...all the minute-by-minute demands on our time.

But, as irresistible people know, we gain so much by just listening 100 percent.

Use "listening body language"

No matter what goal they're after, whether it's a new job, a promotion, more opportunity, a new sale or anything else, irresistible people understand that good listening has a unique set of visual cues. Their "listening body language" sends a clear message: "Right now, nothing of importance is taking place for me except this conversation with you."

Some suggestions for using this powerful idea at work:

- Show the speaker that they have your undivided attention. Clear away distractions. Don't check your phone or fidget with papers in front of you.

- Whether you're standing or sitting, lean in slightly toward the person speaking.

- Keep your expression open: facial muscles relaxed, no frowning.

- Make eye contact to show you're interested and hold the speaker's attention.

- Tilt your head to one side and lift your eyebrows slightly as the speaker is talking.

- Nod at key points, like when the speaker says something interesting or draws a conclusion.

- If appropriate, take notes. People often brighten up when they notice we're writing what they're saying. "It must be important," they think, and feel encouraged to continue.

Taken together, these visual cues and actions send a clear — and irresistible — message: "I'm totally focused on what you're saying. Please keep going!" and they do it more clearly than if we yelled these words out loud!

Watch the speaker's body language...

...it says a lot! In fact, more than 90 percent of a person's message is communicated through their tone of voice and body language. The rest is conveyed through the words they use.

Learning to read these nonverbal cues is essential if we want to really hear – and understand – what someone is trying to say.

So let's pay attention to more than just words: when someone's talking, notice their posture, facial expressions, tone of voice, and gestures.

Is their body language closed and protective (leaning back, arms folded, unsmiling) or open and relaxed (leaning forward, arms and hands relaxed, smiling)? Either way, they're telling us something. As a simple example, someone may say, "Thursday is fine," but if they're saying it with downcast eyes, a pained expression, and slumped shoulders, their body language is contradicting their words (and probably telling the real story).

Is the person making eye contact or looking away? When someone looks directly at us while speaking, chances are they're feeling confident about their topic, comfortable, and happy to talk to us about it. When they look away, the opposite tends to be true.

Tone of voice counts too. How we say what we say – the pace, the volume, energy level in our voice – all communicate more than the words themselves, sometimes much more. So, is the person's voice strong and clear, enthusiastic, and energized? If yes, chances are the subject excites them and their views about it – pro or con – are strong.

On the other hand, a softer, wavering voice may communicate a lack of understanding, commitment, enthusiasm, or confidence in the topic. We can put this speaker at ease by saying, "Maybe we can talk more about this another time?"

Is the person talking very fast? They may just be in a hurry, but there may be more to the story. Fast talking can be a sign of insecurity or discomfort. The person may want to get the conversation over with as fast as possible because they aren't sure of what they're talking about and want to get away before they're asked a question they can't answer.

We can put this speaker at ease with a reassuring: "Okay, that makes sense. Thanks. Looks like you're in a hurry. Maybe we can catch up later?"

"Hearing" a situation

At work, irresistible people have sharp powers of observation, meaning they have learned to "hear" situations as well as conversations.

They take time before a meeting or key conversation to tune in to the people who'll be there and the specific circumstances, mentally asking questions like:

- "Who'll be at this meeting/conference/lunch? Do I know them or anyone who does?"

- "Is there anything I can bring or think about in advance that would be helpful or valuable to people I know will be there?"

- "So that job I really want has been open for six months. That means the company probably hopes to fill the position fast and might be having a tough time finding the right person. Maybe the opening is creating morale problems because employees are overworking to fill the gap. What does all this suggest about the skills I should highlight in the interview? Maybe:

  — 'I work quickly with little direction.'
  — 'I'd have almost no learning curve on this job because of my experience.'

66

> — 'It must be hard to find just the right person for such a crucial job.'"

- "Is this person the actual decisionmaker for the sale I'm trying to make? If yes, I can ask right away for the business. If not, how can I respectfully equip the person to talk about me in positive terms to the actual buyer, maybe:

    > — 'I brought an extra copy of our terms of service if you'd like to share them with Kenna," or "I'm happy to answer any questions Terri may have about my services. Is there anything in particular you think she'd want to know?"

- "I know I'm perfect for this promotion, and I'm eager to bring it up with my manager. But right now, during our busy season, isn't the best time to do that. I'll wait until things calm down."

Each time, the right choice, made after carefully observing the situation, dramatically improves the chances of building strong, irresistible connections to people, not to mention achieving important goals in the bargain.

Out of the question

Questions are a power-packed way to show someone we're listening and steer any conversation in a positive, constructive direction. At work, great questions make us look inquisitive and smart and help build our reputation as a serious and smart person with a genuine interest in the topic at hand and an honest desire to make a situation better.

But too often the right question is an after-the-fact frustration. In *You Know What I ~~Should Have~~ Said?*, I wrote about these moments: we either draw a blank or hesitate, the moment passes, and it's just too late to ask the question we wanted...

"Ugh! You know what I should have asked her?"

"That would have been a good question at the time, but it's too late now."

"The moment was right, but I was afraid my question would make me sound stupid."

We put ourselves under incredible pressure to ask an amazing, brain-busting question like an attorney cross-examining a witness. Absolutely not necessary (and not the tone we want to strike anyway)!

Here are some options we can lock and load to be ready for next time:

To clarify what we're hearing...

- "When you say 'assemble,' do you mean from scratch?"

- "And you said you'll be making a decision next week?"

- "Excuse me, did you say 17 or 70?"

- "Would you tell me again your reason for choosing Johnson HVAC for the warehouse job?"

- "Let me be sure I understand. Do you mean..."

- "Would you explain that to me in layman's terms?"

- "And you said this happened last week? What day?"

To gather information...

- "Who are the key people involved?"

- "What are the company's business goals for this year?"

- "What's been the team's greatest challenge this year? How about its greatest achievement?"

- "When did this begin?"

- "Where will the event take place?"

- "How was that done?"

- "How long did it take you?"

- "How does this job/team contribute to the company's mission?"

- "Why is that goal important to the team?"

- "Why did she decide to ask Sandy's team for help?"

To ask for significance:

- "Would you tell me more about how that would affect the work your team does for the Marketing team?"

- "What does that mean for [*group of people*]?"

- "How will that affect the team?"

- "Will that end up being a positive thing for your team?"

To probe for reasons:

- "Please tell me more about why..."

- "Why did you decide on that approach?"

- "What are the most important reasons you..."

- "I'd really like to hear more about the rationale for that decision."

To interpret what we're hearing:

- "Is that similar to..."

- "What challenges does that create?"

- "What do you expect will happen when..."

- "How does that apply to..."

- "Have you thought about what would happen if..."

To make it real:

- "Can you give me an example?"

- "How would that work in practice?"

- "Are you aware of any statistics on that?"

- "What would need to happen to implement that idea?"

To ask for a prediction or vision:

- "What are next steps in your view?"

- "What do you expect will happen in the next 12 months?"

- "Do you think this would also work in Europe?"

- "I noticed you're opening another distribution center in Tampa. How will this affect current operations?"

Gathering information is only part of the goal of asking questions. The other, sometimes more important goal is to show, just by asking questions and regardless of the answers we get, our irresistibility at work: our interest, genuine excitement, and engagement in the topic. Sometimes, our questions will actually help people think through important issues or spark ideas they didn't even know they had. (Any time we hear someone say, "That's a great question" or "I didn't think of that," we're probably helping them in this way.)

When we ask great questions, our coworkers and managers sense, and rightfully so, that we're thinking through the issues, interested in the topic, and invested in the outcome. That's a magnet that draws positive people and circumstances toward us — the kind of energy everyone wants to be around!

It's — you know — irresistible 😊.

"Who wants to know?"

Some people react to even a mild question with a question of their own: "Why do you want to know?" or "What are you going to do with this information?" or more simply, "Who wants to know?" They're clearly uncomfortable, and this is evident in their word choice as well as, in all likelihood, their tone.

A few tips for managing these reactions:

Remember the audience

Before asking any question, think about their state of mind, needs, and concerns as you shape the question and time the conversation.

Tone really matters

While the ability to ask questions is one of our most powerful communication skills at work, discretion is a must. Again, some people just react to any question as a threat or a challenge to their skills or credibility. So we need to be sure we don't sound like we're on a fact-finding mission for the CIA — "Where were you on the night of the 13th?!" — and instead, ask questions with a mild tone that conveys curiosity, interest, or need to know.

When we anticipate resistance, we can lower the chance of a defensive reaction by starting questions with phrases like:

- "I was hoping to find out…"

- "Would it be possible to talk about…"

- "I was wondering if we could review…"

- "First of all, thanks so much for taking the time to talk to me about this…"

Follow through

Irresistible people help any speaker relax by showing they've heard correctly, thanking them, and providing reassurances they'll follow through on what they've heard.

Three steps:

Confirm/clarify

- "I want to be sure I heard you correctly. Did you say..."

- "Is it fair to say you mean..."

- "I see, so you're concerned about..."

- "So what you're hoping for is..."

- "So you'd like me to..."

- "The one thing you want to be sure everyone knows is..."

- "And the one thing you want to be certain doesn't happen is..."

Say thanks

- "Thanks for explaining that to me."

- "I appreciate you sharing this with me."

- "I really value your thinking/input/ideas on this."

Explain how you'll follow through

- "I'll definitely look into that and let you know."

- "I see where you're coming from. Do you have some time to talk more about that idea?"

- "Sounds interesting. Let me give it some thought/do some research/talk to Jim's team and get back to you."

Encourage the speaker

As they listen, irresistible people know how to reassure the person who's speaking, helping them feel relaxed and comfortable, plus more open to share their ideas and willing to hear feedback in return.

As you're listening and when it makes sense to do so (not annoyingly often — just once every couple of minutes!), nod and say —

- "Yes, I see."

- "I hear what you're saying."

- "I understand what you mean."

- "What happened next?"

- "Can you tell me more about..."

- "You're an expert on this. I respect your ideas."

- "I understand your reaction."

Irresistible people know that absolutely everyone craves this kind of validation. It literally floods a person with good feelings to know that we're paying attention, we understand, and most of all that we respect them enough to hear them out.

They're far more willing to listen when it's our turn to talk and more receptive to our ideas — even dissenting ideas — when we do.

Let them finish!

Interrupting someone to complete their sentences can feel really disrespectful. First, it creates a vibe that says, "I know what you're going to say" which short circuits their thinking. It also says, intentionally or not, that we think the speaker is so predictable — so incapable of an original idea — that we can actually complete their thoughts for them.

As someone's about to say, "I called and Simone said the group would be ready to go on Thursday, unless —"

The listener jumps in, "Unless there are any more changes from us."

"Actually no," says the speaker.

"Oh, you mean unless money is an issue."

"No," says the speaker, annoyed now.

"I know, unless other people want to join in."

"What I'm trying to say is, unless there are more problems with the supplier!"

Worst case, the speaker might just stop in frustration and think, "Obviously you know what I'm going to say, so why should I even bother talking at all?"

We can even complete someone's sentences in our own minds. It may look like we're listening, but we're not. Why bother when we know what they're going to say? No need to waste the time actually listening!

Maybe as we're listening, we start to plan how we'll respond, and as we do, we miss part, maybe even a critical part, of what the person is trying to say.

We also miss the chance to connect with the speaker and build or strengthen our work relationship. Author Stephen Covey once said, "Most people do not listen with the intent to understand; they listen with the intent to reply."

So let's follow the example of irresistible people and let the speaker finish what they need to say, even if we disagree, and even if we already know what they're going to say.

Beautiful someone, this aspect of listening is more important to our irresistibility than we may realize!

Listen past the quirks

It's easy to be thrown off by someone's communication style, especially if we find it annoying or hard to follow. We get busy counting someone's "ums" and "uhs" or distracted by how fast or slowly they talk or by their too-big gestures or too-loud voice. And in the process, we totally miss the point they're trying to make.

Not everyone is a great communicator, and even people who are can be so pressed for time that they don't have the energy to finesse what they're saying or deliver it politely in the moment.

Some people are naturally blunt; others are indirect.

Some are so talkative that they tend to bury us in detail we don't need.

Some are defensive. Others are easygoing.

Some are dramatic while others are so bland that we struggle to stay awake.

But at some point, we have to work with all of them!

If we listen past someone's quirky style, not only will we hear their full message, we'll realize that pretty much everyone has something unique and valuable to add to the conversation. Beneath the gruffness or too-loud voice, there's something worth listening to, and hearing it gives us real power: greater variety of ideas and more information, more contacts, a stronger network.

And, as a bonus, more people willing to hear us out when it's our turn to talk.

So let's work at not letting these quirky styles interfere with our ability to fully hear what people have to say.

Result: us — more irresistible by the day.

DIANA DAVIN

"

One of the sincerest forms
of respect is actually listening
to what someone has to say.

— Bryant H. McGill

"

Talk so people will listen...

Share your ideas
Let them know you

Irresistible people work hard at conversations. They start and keep good dialogue going — even when it stalls, even when it's hard — and learn something valuable about themselves and other people in the process. Easy, comfortable conversations are high priority for them.

Be heard, get noticed

"Nothing haunts us like
the things we *don't* say."

— Mitch Albom

Speaking up at work is a risk. Using our voices to share ideas, ask questions, chance a guess...all this and more makes us visible and accountable for what we say. When we speak up, our reputation takes shape.

People look at us, and eventually *to* us, for information, advice, or support. Some will agree with us; others won't. Some will like us, others not so much. Some will encourage us, others will challenge or disagree with us. And everyone will form their opinions of our intelligence, skill, personality (my hands are sweating!) based on what we say.

It's easy to understand why taking the initiative to share an idea, start a conversation, or even just ask a question can feel death-defying at times. It really can seem so much easier to just quietly blend in with the wallpaper.

And yet...who really wants to be wallpaper at work? Comfortable in the background where it's safe, but not much else? Living with the frustration that comes with, "Oh man, you know what I should have said" or "I should have asked that when I had the chance"? (Beautiful someone, read much more about getting out ahead of these situations in my book, *You Know What I ~~Should Have~~ Said?* with strategies for speaking up in both our personal and work lives.)

Not us! So we nix the "shoulds" and boost our irresistibility, share our ideas, and let people get to know us — by speaking up.

Irresistible people are willing to talk to anyone at any time about anything. They work hard to start a conversation and keep it going, regardless of how nervous they feel or how communicative the other person may (or may not!) be.

They have successful conversations with coworkers who are blunt or indirect, talkative or quiet, monosyllabic ("Yes," "No," "Good," "Worse") or chatty, thoughtful or super-opinionated.

Here's how all this boosts our irresistibility

As we take the initiative to speak up, we encourage the people around us — colleagues, coworkers, clients, teammates — to feel comfortable doing the same, sharing their ideas, asking questions, telling stories. We radiate an open vibe, a sense that we're willing to share our thoughts in any professional setting and listen to others' too.

Plus, our conversation skills help us ease into any situation — regardless of the topic — and make ourselves and others relaxed and comfortable. We speak up, extend a hand in greeting, introduce and connect people to each other, share ideas and, yes, risk getting a thumbs-down!

Speaking up *does* take courage, beautiful someone. Behind the outgoing nature and the hand extended to meet a new colleague (and in spite of the smile and the open expression they wear), irresistible people are often feeling uncomfortable, awkward, and sometimes just plain afraid. They may struggle for the right things to say. They've probably embarrassed themselves once or twice by saying the wrong thing at the wrong time. And like pretty much everybody else, they'd rather be at the café with friends or at home with family who love them no matter what.

But irresistible people know that as they make the effort to share their ideas, take part in the meeting, cool conflicts, and smooth over rough spots with the right words, they'll be remembered in positive ways. So they're not willing to let their fears and discomfort limit them.

They won't let themselves hang out in safe, unchallenging places. They refuse to give up on their dreams and the connections and visibility those dreams depend on. They won't be defeated or walk away from a situation weighed down with regret over what they should have said and knowing they could have done much better if they'd just asked the question or said what was on their minds.

Irresistible people make the effort to speak up because they know it's worth it for them and the people around them.

Fortunately, speaking up gets easier with practice, and we even start to groove on the surge of power we feel when we're dropped into an unfamiliar situation with people we don't know, but have the communication skills and confidence to navigate our way easily and end the moment stronger than we were before, with even more loyal colleagues and coworkers.

Let's take speaking up off our list of work skills to strengthen!

Irresistible conversation

First, we breathe!

When we're nervous in a situation, we tend to overthink things, putting way too much pressure on ourselves. Few conversations are truly life-altering with permanent consequences. Most are just momentary touches that quickly fade. This means that even if a meeting or conversation isn't going as well as we'd like, there's a good chance the person we're talking to is already distracted by the next thing on their list.

So if you're nervous or uncomfortable before a particular conversation, take a moment first to breathe and consciously relax:

Sit up straight: lengthen your upper body from the base of your spine all the way through to the crown of your head (imagine a crown being placed on your head, beautiful someone).

Take a few deep breaths — really big ones that fill your chest and upper back.

Relax your shoulders. Let them drop and roll them back a few times slowly.

Let your face soften, relaxing the muscles in your jaw and forehead.

Open your hands and shake them gently.

Flex your fingers a few times.

Picture yourself in a place that makes you feel calm: the beach, the woods, a theater...

Relaxing in these ways lets us keep perspective and has the added benefit of helping us focus. As we deliberately calm down, we clear our mind and concentrate our energy on the dialogue we're about to have, which can't help but be better and more irresistible as a result!

Positive possibilities

"Desire," wrote 16th Century mathematician René Descartes, "awakens only to things that are thought possible." There's a chapter in my book, *Dream Come True*, called "Look for what you want to find." I was trying to make the point that we "find" or rather that we create what we're looking for, what we focus on and, most of all, believe is possible. (Same idea, even if it's not as eloquent as Descartes!)

This idea of finding what we're looking for applies to all parts of life, including work. When we focus on positive possibilities, we sharpen our vision, attune our hearing, and literally move our feet in the direction of what we want and believe we can achieve – all the good stuff.

Let's use this to our irresistible advantage at work by setting the greatest expectations for our next conversation, telling ourselves:

"I can handle this conversation, and it will go well."

"I'm going to enjoy this discussion."

"I'm expecting great things to come out of this meeting. We're going to resolve the most important issues and leave with clear action steps."

"The prospect is going to be much more comfortable with the new terms I've included in the contract. I'm confident she'll sign this week."

"After we talk, Geoff will introduce me to the right people at the conference."

A quick note about having great expectations: some people may say they sound "unrealistic." So what? It doesn't matter. It's better to set great expectations and come close to reaching them than it is to set low expectations and meet them.

We're making positive changes here, beautiful someone, and that takes hope and belief in a better future. We'll take the "unrealistic" label.

It actually feels just right.

Prep for important conversations

The negotiation for that once-in-a-lifetime opportunity

The performance review and bonus discussion

The key interview for the hoped-for job

The meeting with executives who'll decide if it's worth moving ahead with your project

Irresistible people never begin critical conversations like these unprepared. They do their homework in advance, get some details on the people who'll be there, and then memorize conversation starters, talking points, questions they want to ask, and answers to questions they think they'll be asked.

In addition to ensuring that they're ready to maximize the conversation and make strong connections to the people who'll be there, the discipline of preparation puts everyone at ease. When irresistible people are fully prepared for a conversation, they prevent uncomfortable gaps in the dialogue and reassure everyone present that the conversation will stay focused and go smoothly.

Let's follow their example:

Schedule critical conversations with enough lead time to get ready.

Research the topic fully, so you're fully aware of the history, key facts, trends, latest developments, etc.

Prepare a few conversation starters about the weather, sports, or headlines (nothing political or controversial!).

Memorize a handful of talking points – essential, key ideas that you want to be sure make it into the conversation.

Anticipate the questions you may be asked (especially the tough ones) and prep solid answers. Try them out on a coworker or friend who understands the situation.

Think about any objections the person you're talking to might have about your topic or your request and prepare smart responses.

The one thing

Irresistible people make sure that important conversations, meetings, phone calls, and emails have a purpose, and this gives their communication focus and energy. They never start a critical conversation without a firm handle on their "one thing," which is simply this:

*If the people involved in this conversation
forget everything else, what's the one thing
I want them to remember?*

The answer to this key question is both more important and harder than we think! But it also gives us the confidence that comes from knowing the direction we'd like things to take and enables us to steer the conversation accordingly. Our energy and confidence are attractive to the people around us who conclude (rightfully!) that we're knowledgeable; we know our subject or hold firmly to our point of view.

And there's more. Knowing what we want to accomplish in a given situation:

Helps us get to the point faster because we know what the point *is*.

Puts our listeners at ease by reassuring them that we won't go on and on (and on!), a huge plus at a time when attention spans at work are shorter than ever.

Actually helps us finish a conversation having achieved something specific.

So, in advance, let's decide on the "one thing" that will let us walk away from a conversation thinking, "I aced that one!" What do we want the other person or group to realize or understand when the conversation ends?

Be precise!

"I want the group to believe that my five-step approach will start saving us at least 10 hours of overtime a week right away."

"I want the prospect to see that my offer is unique in these three ways..."

"I want the group to understand and agree with the top two reasons we should open an office in London in the next 12 months."

"I want my manager to remember my dedication and hard work in the last year, including my willingness to cover for people who called out on the weekends."

Then, we can get even more specific — what would we like our listeners to think or say by the time the conversation ends?

"I agree."

"I see your point."

"That makes sense."

"Yes, let's..."

"Sure thing. I'll..."

"Here's the information you needed."

"I'm with you. Let's get started."

"You got the job!"

"Where do I sign?"

"What's in it for me?"

It's a thought that forms automatically in everyone's mind when we open our Inbox and start reading, sit down for a meeting, or take part in any conversation: "Why should I bother to read or listen to this? Why is this worth my time?"

We want clear and convincing answers before we devote our precious time and energy to anything.

Let's turn the tables and take a close look at the person or group we're talking to. Read the thought bubble over their head that says, "Why should I care?" and be prepared to answer from their perspective, based on their needs:

"Because what I'm going to tell you will —

help you _____."

get you ready for _____."

show the advantages of _____."

show you how we can _____."

share strategies we can use to _____."

let you jumpstart _____."

help us get out ahead of _____."

When our conversations begin and end with our audience's interests, we will for sure be heard — every time!

Plugged in

Scanning the headlines is a great daily discipline that helps us feel plugged in to what's happening in the world. And, it helps us create irresistible conversation: even if we just spend a few minutes looking at the weather forecast, movie news, bestselling books and sports highlights, we have conversation openers or topics to spark or fill gaps in any conversation.

We'll also be less likely to find ourselves at a loss for words when someone mentions an important headline or current event, especially something that impacts our company, key competitors, or industry.

So bookmark news pages, subscribe to feeds and set up alerts about general news as well as news relevant to your company and your job.

In addition to helping us prepare for conversations of all kinds, plugging in makes it easy to say, "Oh yeah, I did read about that" or "Did you see the clip about..." or "I saw that headline!" in a conversation, or to easily answer someone who asks, "Hey, what do you think about ABC Company downsizing?"

This practice will also keep us current on important developments affecting business and enable us to link any topic of work conversation to current events affecting our company or industry.

Irresistible? Oh yeah!

Back-pocket a few questions as starters

The best conversation starters are simple. Questions work well because they invite conversation.

Relax and just be friendly and polite:

"When did you join the company?"
"What team are you with?"
"Where are you located?"

Other work-appropriate conversation starters are local sports team wins, upcoming business trips, or even headlines about a bestselling book or movie: "There's all this buzz about [*recent bestseller or movie*]. Have you read/seen it?"

If you're at an event, another option is to talk about the gathering itself: the setting, the food, the occasion, the weather (yes, talking about the weather is cliché, but it works!):

"Good to meet you! How do you know [*the person or group hosting the event*]?"

"What an amazing place! Have you ever been here before?"

"Wow, did you see the buffet?"

More general questions can be good too:

"What's keeping you busy these days?"

"Are you enjoying the summer?"

"Any special plans for the holidays?"

"I'm trying to plan a winter trip. Any suggestions?"

Quick word of caution: no matter how breezily we ask, some people get defensive about being asked questions, even if all we ask is, "When did you join the company?"

They may respond with, "Who wants to know?" or "Why exactly do you need to know?"

It's impossible to understand why someone reacts this way to a simple question. They may have a history of working with prying people or like to keep a strong line between work and personal life that they feel we're trying to cross. They could be facing relationship or family problems...or any one of a long list of other issues.

We may never know, and really, it doesn't matter. Most of all, we shouldn't get defensive too. If we try several ways to engage someone in conversation, and they're clearly not interested, let them be. Move on with smile and a simple, "Good to meet you. See you later."

Then graciously exit.

Share something

Sometimes, we can put someone at ease by first volunteering some information about ourselves. ("I come from a family of people with interesting careers — my Dad is a pastry chef and my Mom is a sculptor — so I'm always curious about people whose jobs sound fascinating" or "You're from Massachusetts? I live in Westfield, but I grew up in a small town called Granville. Have you heard of it?").

Sharing a bit of information about ourselves can put people at ease. They may not realize it consciously, but when we're more open with other people, they are more likely to feel more trusting and comfortable opening up and sharing with us.

...a light and easy give-and-take that's at the very heart of irresistibility in conversation!

See what they see

When someone needs directions to our house, the first thing we ask is, "Where are you coming from?" We've got to know the person's starting point in order to give them directions from where *they* are to where *we* are.

Irresistible conversation works the same way. To make a solid connection to another person, we need to know where they're "coming from" on our topic (how they feel about it, what they know, what matters to them about it). When our starting point is telling people what *they* need to know rather than what *we* want to say, we become totally irresistible: credible professionals who can be counted on for information people rely on as having their interests at heart.

Our conversation becomes irresistible because we attract others with ideas we know will appeal to them. We also save time and effort. As we speak the language of their needs and concerns, people naturally tune in (wouldn't you? ☺), and our struggle to get them to hear us over the general noise of the work day ends. They're confident we understand what matters to them, and that makes them interested in what we have to say.

We can be better prepared for any conversation by thinking about the audience: standing in their shoes, hearing with their ears, and seeing with their eyes:

What do they already know about the topic? Have they been waiting for news on this topic?

How do they feel about the topic? How deeply involved are they? How much of a stake do they have in it...how important is it to them? What opinions do they have about the type of information under discussion?

What's happening for them right now: A new job, a long-hoped-for promotion, a crucial deadline? If they're in the middle of a work crisis, how are things going? What challenges are they facing: job pressures, budget problems, significant change, reassignment?

What's their work style? Do they like lots of detail, want just the high points of an idea, or something in-between? Do they value teamwork and delegation or do their best work alone? Are they experienced professionals or novices?

What objections could they have to the topic? Are there any points they're likely to resist? Is your message controversial in any way? How can your message be shaped to avoid confrontation?

What are they expecting to find out right now? In a job interview, what aspects of your background will interest the interviewer most? In the middle of a project, what type of help might a colleague need to finish? What is your manager waiting to hear from you? What result is your customer hoping for?

Beautiful someone, as we do this quality of in-depth thinking about our audience, our irresistibility takes a quantum leap. Who could resist listening to us when we've taken the time to understand where they're coming from and know just what they need to hear, when, and how? Who could disagree with us when we know what to highlight or downplay when we talk?

What works

A simple idea that can really help boost irresistible conversation: rehearse your conversation skills in no-risk situations like family get-togethers, time with friends, or community projects. Speaking up in these low-key situations can be a great learning experience as you take note of:

What worked, what didn't?

When were you most comfortable?

What made you *un*comfortable?

What skills do you want to sharpen to look/feel more confident?

And practice is its own reward: as we try out our skills in low-risk situations, we build confidence, getting more comfortable with speaking up and more relaxed about doing it in other settings.

Spice

It's easier to attract attention for our message — and make it more memorable — when we season it with words that add originality and style, words like *tenacity, vibrant, peak, energize, breakthrough, dynamic, enterprising, vital, bravo, surge, surefire, fuel, vivid,* and *exceptional.*

At the same time (and for the same reason!), try to avoid clichés like "at the end of the day," "day in and day out" and "in leaps and bounds." People tune these phrases out because the words have lost meaning through overuse. (They may even get so distracted by them that they'll start counting the number of times we use each one!)

Let's give our irresistibility a charge by communicating like the unique and original businesspeople we are.

Bravo!

Pacing

Irresistible professionals manage the pace of conversation with skillful use of open- and closed-ended questions.

Open-ended questions are requests for ideas or information that slow the pace of a conversation by sparking discussion, for example:

"What's your experience with..."

"What did you enjoy most about..."

"What are the most important reasons you..."

"What would your reaction be if..."

"Why is that alternative viable in your view?"

"What needs to happen next?"

Answers to questions like these will be detailed and thoughtful, the start of a longer dialogue. In this way, these questions are useful for slowing the conversation down and provoking discussion.

On the other hand, closed-ended questions pick up the pace by asking for a brief, definitive answer, for example:

"How long will it take to..."

"Would you say that..."

"Do you agree with Jon?"

"What time are we starting?"

"Was Bryan there?"

"Who will be presenting?"

Answers to these questions will be short and simple: "A few days," "Yes," "No," "At 3:00 today."

It's easy to see how skilled use of open- and closed-ended questions enables irresistible people (that would be us!) to control the pace of conversation in positive ways.

Raise a hand

Irresistible people do a lot of volunteering. Raising their hand to get involved or take on more work or responsibility draws them into experiences that create new connections and career breakthroughs. Being willing to get involved also exposes them to cutting-edge ideas and builds relationships with the people who generate them.

A few ideas for following their lead:

Participate in mentoring programs that enable you to give back to the next generation by supporting them with advice and information you've earned in your career.

Raise a hand to lead or participate in special projects or task forces that put you on the leading edge of your company's direction and industry position.

Volunteer to speak at in-house meetings and even industry conferences representing your company.

Speaking body language

"I wonder if Mari knows how severe she looks with that expression on her face. It's really distracting."

The comment was whispered in the middle of a meeting but carried a clear message about the manager's impression of Mari's abilities and potential.

When we're speaking, our facial expressions, gestures, and even our tone of voice communicate a lot, more than the words we use. Irresistible people make sure these visual cues are sending the right message:

A pointed finger, even when it's being used to encourage or agree with someone, is a sharp and direct gesture that can be uncomfortable for many people. In contrast, an open hand is inviting and welcoming. Best to gesture toward someone with an open hand, palm facing up to refer to them or include their idea.

Unless sub-zero temperatures have chilled you to the bone, keep your arms unwrapped. Don't bundle them in front of your chest in a tight posture that can say, "I'm uncomfortable," "I don't believe you," "I disagree with you," "I'm bored," "You're wasting my time..."

Be aware of the subliminal message your voice is sending. A voice with positive energy is irresistible to listeners. Breathe deeply and keep your voice clear and strong to convey clarity and confidence. People react by feeling comfortable and confident around you. Consciously or not, they think, "She sounds so sure of herself, she obviously knows what she's talking about, so what she's saying must be true and accurate."

Style matching

Jana is a successful interior designer who works with clients to bring their dream homes to life. She credits her success to one thing: her ability to adapt her communication style to match her clients'.

"If I didn't know how to make people feel comfortable," she says, "I mean I'm in their homes talking about their personal space, right? – I don't think I'd be successful at this job. It definitely helps when I adapt my communication style to theirs. That's the key to making people comfortable, putting them at ease so they can open up and freely express their dreams to me."

An executive at a pharmaceutical company has an amazing gift for talking to anyone, any time. When she's with employees in a relaxed and chatty setting, her style automatically shifts to match. When she's in a formal setting with a scientific audience, she's buttoned up and formal. In both cases, and in every situation in between, she's using a powerful strategy to encourage her employees and colleagues to open up around her and work together.

Matching someone's style makes the person comfortable listening and talking to us. They feel — and it *is* a feeling, not an intellectual decision — as if they're talking to someone just like them, someone who understands them. There is a sense of mutual understanding. The person relaxes, speaks more openly, and listens to us more closely. The more relaxed they are, the more likely they are to share their ideas, and the more likely they are to listen to ours.

This is irresistible magic, beautiful someone, and it's so simple!

When we're with someone who is talkative and informal for example, we can shift our style to match.

If, on the other hand, the person is more formal or speaks more deliberately, we can do the same.

If someone is more comfortable speaking slowly, let's do the same.

If they talk fast, we should skip the detail, cut to the chase, and talk fast.

If they're "all business," we can mirror that style, eliminating small talk and sticking to the facts and data.

Another way to match styles and put a listener at ease: reflect their unique word choice back to them. For example, if someone uses a certain phrase such as, "in the final analysis" or "high potential," picking up on that phrase and using it ourselves once or twice enables the person to feel heard and validated.

Importantly, matching styles is not about parroting someone's words or movements. Rather it's a way to make a person comfortable talking to us by sending them a subtle message that we understand them and have a similar point of view and approach to solving problems. As a result, the person is more likely to be receptive to our ideas...and to us.

As we actively demonstrate through our tone and body language that we understand the person's needs and concerns, walls come down, bridges are built, and soon, we're on the solid (and irresistible!) ground of mutual respect and understanding.

When to <u>stop</u> talking
Have you ever been trapped in a conversation with someone who just talks and talks?

"Oh, hey, Josh, how are you? I *did* have a chance to look at those figures, the ones that Sophie sent over last Thursday afternoon—no, no, I think it was morning, yes, morning, somewhere before 10 because I always get my second cup of coffee at 10 and I remember I hadn't done that yet. I'm really glad you called because now we can finally discuss them, which is helpful because they did come out of that new process Jack and his team designed last year when that whole area was being restructured, which I think was finished in maybe June, maybe July or thereabouts. We can talk about them right now, let's see, it's what? 2:30. Yes, now's fine with me...I don't have any meetings this afternoon, except well, I've got something very briefly to go to at 3:00 — it's with Jo, Sierra and Alex, and we're just supposed to quickly touch base on that systems proposal we've been working on for the last four months. As I said, I think that should only take about ten minutes, but you never know, heh heh, these things tend to run on and on...."

Your eyes glaze over and you start to get restless as you think of the thousand things you need to be (or would rather be) doing.

This is an exaggerated example to make a point, but it's easy, especially when we have to pay attention to so many things at once and move fast between priorities, to "overstay our welcome" in someone's schedule. In fact, it doesn't take much at all.

Irresistible people are hyper-aware of social cues that indicate how their audience is reacting to their message, and never let themselves lose their listeners.

How can we tell we're losing our listeners?

The other person hasn't spoken in a minute or more.

The person's body language is getting restless; maybe they're starting to fidget.

They've started to angle away or look around the room.

Their eyes are glazing over, and they look bored and disengaged.

They seem impatient enough to cut in and ask, "What's your point?"

If you sense your audience drifting, finish! Move right away to: "And my point is..." or "The bottom line is..." or "From a practical perspective, this means..." or "Here's how this would work for you, Zoe." You might also ask the person a question: "Have you had a similar experience?" "Do you know what I mean?" "So tell me, what's new with you? How's your job/work/project going?"

When we have a balanced approach to give and take, talk and listen in conversation, people find us irresistible because beneath the surface (and sometimes without even realizing it consciously), they trust us to respect their time and priorities. They're not afraid to engage in conversation with us and even share their ideas openly because we've put them at ease. They know they'll be heard and respected but not overburdened with listening to us for longer than they want to.

Shorter is sharper

A search for quotes on brevity will get thousands of results, including this one from 32nd U.S. President Franklin Delano Roosevelt: "Be sincere. Be brief. Be seated."

Irresistible people don't make the mistake of thinking that sounding sophisticated requires using as many words as possible. Especially to the ear (as opposed to the eye through reading), wordiness just bores people and wastes their time.

In every conversation, there are lots of opportunities to cut out extra words...

Instead of the wordy...	We can just say...
During the course of	During
Few in number	Few
Get together for a meeting	Meet
Qualified expert	Expert
Throughout the entire	Throughout
Very unique	Unique
Shows a preference for	Prefers
Completely eliminated	Eliminated
File away	File
Prolong the duration	Prolong
Come to the realization	Realize
Green in color	Green
On a daily basis	Daily
On a regular basis	Regularly
Make a decision	Decide
In order that	So

An "irresistible" endpoint to shorter is sharper: William Zinsser, author of *On Writing Well* wrote, "There's not much to be said about the period except that most writers don't reach it soon enough."

When in doubt...

Beautiful someone, language is a powerful tool that can cause serious damage when used improperly. Sensitivity is key.

If we find ourselves wondering whether something could offend a person or a group, our best bet is not to risk it.

In general at work: 1) avoid conversations about politics, religion, and personal relationships, and 2) when in doubt, leave it out.

And just a quick note on the dicey stuff: ever have a work conversation with someone who stands too close, or even worse, touches you as they talk? Though this can be an unconscious and benign habit of trying to engage you or tapping you on the arm to punctuate a point, it's a form of "space invasion" that distracts the listener and detracts from the speaker's effectiveness.

Needless to say, touching of any kind at work can be considered unwelcome and inappropriate, and thus have even more serious consequences.

So, at work, irresistible people keep their distance and are definitely completely and totally hands off.

"

It took me quite a long time to
develop a voice, and now that I have it,
I am not going to be silent.

— Madeleine Albright

"

Keep your word...

Show your integrity
Build their trust

Irresistible professionals are consistent and reliable. They're on time. They meet deadlines. Keep promises. Their "yes" means "yes," and their "no" means "no," and they are completely consistent about this. They are trusted and sought after. Anyone who works with them knows exactly what to expect, and they are never disappointed.

Be trusted — and sought after

"Be real. Do what you say,
say what you mean, and
be what you seem."

— Marian Wright Edelman

"I trust you."

That's got to be one of the best compliments we can ever get. This compliment takes many forms at work:

"I totally trust Gina's answer on this subject."

"If Ana says it, you know it's true."

"If Jason promised he'd get it done, he will."

"Hanna will be on time. You can set your watch by her."

"If there's anyone we can trust to solve this problem, it's Ben."

Trustworthiness is high on the list of qualities irresistible people have in abundance. Because of their utter dependability, they are sought after, listened to, respected, and on everyone's mind in positive ways when good opportunities come up.

Being trustworthy is the very definition of having *integrity* which literally means showing strength through wholeness and cohesion. Integrity is being honest and having strong principles, but also being whole and undivided. Integrity at work

117

means doing the right thing and also being a person of our word: consistent, reliable, and principled.

It's interesting too that when we're considered trustworthy, people won't want to disappoint us. Drawn to our integrity, they will want to return in kind. When our actions lift them up in this way, they will want to play on the field where we define the positive, empowering, and future-focused rules of engagement.

Super simple
Being trustworthy is really just doing all the things that let people count on us and relax when we say something will happen. First and foremost, it's keeping our word — showing up when we say we will, meeting deadlines, delivering what we promised, doing what we say we'll do — so people know if we say it, it's totally reliable.

And there's more...

Being trustworthy is doing a job right down to the smallest details (so people can count on us to deliver quality).

It's refusing to sugarcoat the truth but instead being honest and — this is key — doing it in a supportive, balanced way (so if we say it, we mean it).

It's authenticity, being a WYSIWG (what-you-see-is-what-you-get) person (so people never have to guess what our real agenda is, and they can relax and be open and genuine around us).

Being trustworthy is never taking part in gossip (so people can trust us not to talk about them when they're not around).

It's focusing on the bright side, the positive possibilities in a bad situation (so people know they can rely on us to find the silver lining that makes things better).

Listen for themes of consistency, honesty, loyalty, and positive energy, plus dependability, empathy, and putting others or the team first.

When people trust us at work, they relax around us. They know they can safely make decisions based on our word. When we say we'll be there, we are. When we say something will be finished, it is, and every *i* is dotted and *t* is crossed. They can set their next steps accordingly, knowing our contributions are solid. If they tell us something in confidence, they know for sure it will stay that way. It will go no further.

Some of this may sound simple. "Of course, all that's so obvious," we think. "You have to keep your word and show up on time." But as anyone who's been working for more than five minutes knows (including the truly irresistible people who've mastered this skill!), in the real world, it's not easy to keep our word every time, be consistently authentic, never gossip — especially when we're being pulled in by coworkers and are afraid of being judged as "antisocial" if we don't take part — and always find a silver lining in a tough situation.

But when we master the secrets of building our trustworthiness and protecting it passionately, we're influential, respected, invited into the inner circle, taken seriously, and sought after...a more valuable member of any team.

The key, the real reason irresistible people can be counted on to...

- Do exactly what they say they'll do

- Be there when they say they will

- Lend a hand when they can help

- Do an excellent job

- Call when they say they will

- Meet deadlines

- Send the information they promised

...is that they know a few secrets.

Let's take a closer look.

Building irresistible trust

Commit with care

More than in any other part of life, at work we want to give the impression that, whatever is asked of us, we can handle it! No deadline, new priority, or change in how we do our job can throw us off. And this is where we risk getting in trouble by overcommitting, not being honest with ourselves about how much we can realistically get done in the time available...and in all ways, make commitments we know we can definitely keep.

Irresistible people are super-careful to manage the expectations people have of them. The goal is to be sure they don't overestimate what they can accomplish, fall short, and disappoint people in the process. They don't overextend themselves so they're never in the position of being so rushed that they miss details, forget to return calls and emails or overlook the needs of other people. They give themselves enough of a time-and-energy margin that they're not forced to back out of commitments because they're so overwhelmed that they just can't do it all.

Our turn...

A simple first step to committing with care (i.e., managing the expectations people have of us) is to be ultra-clear about what we can and will do. Before making any commitment, let's pause to ask ourselves first and foremost, whether this is a request we *should* fulfill? Is it right, good, valuable? Does it further a worthwhile goal or serve another positive purpose?

If it passes those tests, then we need to think about some other questions:

"Do I have the energy to deliver on this commitment with excellence and quality?"

"Can I actually fit one more thing into my schedule?"

"If I say yes, will my other priorities suffer?"

"Can I make it to that appointment on time, prepared, relaxed and ready?"

"Am I already committed to other things that are more important?"

"Is this just too ambitious? Will I be able to complete this with consistent energy, or will I start with enthusiasm, but then give up in exhaustion?"

We can take a close look at our answers and then commit only to what we're absolutely sure we can deliver.

Like this...

- Give yourself *more* time than you think you'll need to be on time and prepared for a meeting or ace a deadline.

- Leave at least a 30-minute margin (plus whatever travel time you may need) between appointments.

- Rather than schedule hour-long meetings, make them 45 minutes so you have 15 minutes to regroup and prepare for the next one.

- Schedule "down time" so you can think and regroup for your next challenge.

- *Under*estimate what you can accomplish in 24 hours. Cut your daily To-Do list by a third.

- Glance at your calendar at the start of the week to see where your appointments are concentrated and how the week looks so you can "big picture" budget your time and energy.

- If your time is already stretched, tell the client who's asking for her report by Tuesday that you can have it done by Friday. (If you finish by Wednesday or Thursday, the client will be delighted. If not, she'll be satisfied when it arrives on Friday. Delighted or satisfied...but never disappointed!)

- Ask questions until you're absolutely clear about the scope and timing of every element of an assignment or request: "What exactly needs to be done and when?" "How high a priority is the request?" "Who else is involved?" "Is a specific event driving this deadline?"

- If you're a contractor or gig worker, no matter how urgent a project or order is, don't start until you've got a contract that details exactly what you'll deliver, by when and at what cost, plus any expenses you'll bill.

Goal-aware

Believe it or not, understanding where we're headed in our careers is essential to building strong trust in any work situation or relationship. When we know our priorities and they are a firm and clear part of our work lives, we can be sure that the commitments we make align with these goals.

Just as important, we're much less likely to make commitments that *don't* match our goals (the kind we either can't or don't want to keep). We're less likely to make a promise in a rush, without giving it enough thought, often to satisfy someone else or avoid an uncomfortable "no" moment rather than because the promise aligns with goals we value. When the time comes to follow through on a promise like this, we struggle because it won't move us forward toward goals that matter to us. It may even be counterproductive for us.

But when we know our goals, we can distinguish the activities that are worth time and attention from those that aren't. We don't commit to the wrong things and risk disappointing people by being unable to deliver. Knowing our goals also enables us to consistently keep our commitments because they are promises we value and believe in.

This is not at all to say that we never do things unless we want to. That's a sure road to a self-involved, lackluster career. Plenty of assignments, meetings, conversations, and calls are command performances, and we're there whether we want to be or not. We know how important it is to show up for them with a smile and an open attitude of, "Hey, you know I just might have something to learn in this situation," or "I could meet someone interesting or important here, and I intend to be open to that possibility."

But in all other cases, we need to take care that the commitments we make are aligned with our goals. That means of course that we need to know what those goals *are*. Where do we want to be in the next two years? Five years? What steps so we need to take (courses, certifications, connections, online presence, etc.) to reach our goals?

Goal-setting food for thought:

- ❑ Title/position I will achieve...

- ❑ Company or business I will work for...

- ❑ Promotion I will receive...

- ❑ Location where I will work...

- ❑ Clients or customers I will attract...

- ❑ Skills I will strengthen...

- ❑ People I will develop...

- ❑ Income I will earn...

- ❑ Work/life balance I will achieve...

- ❑ Business relationships I will foster or strengthen...

- ❑ Visibility and networking I will take advantage of...

- ❑ Awards/recognition I will receive...

- ❑ Other areas in which I will achieve...

Clear standards

The top research scientist at a global pharmaceutical company used these words to describe his division's General Manager: "You can trust her. Her goals are right out there, very clear, and you always know where you stand with her. Believe it or not, that makes me optimistic, even when the news isn't good. I can't tell you the stress this takes out of my otherwise demanding job here."

Irresistible! When everyone in our circle knows precisely what they need to do to succeed with us as well as the standards and expectations we have of ourselves, our credibility and influence increase. They know they can relax around us because we have no hidden agenda...what they see is what they get. That's a lot less stress for them, and they know it.

Email!

By helping to minimize the possibility for confusion, any form of clear communication creates trust as it clarifies expectations and helps ensure everyone is on the same page. This is where email is an absolute star.

In email, we have a powerful trust-building tool. Email creates an immediate and permanent record of a conversation, contract, report, invoice, or any other document, and makes it easy to follow the thread of a negotiation or agreement-in-the-making.

We can use email to be sure everyone fully understands what we're committing to, by when, and if applicable, at what cost. Specifically, email can enable us to:

- Confirm project steps

- Schedule or recap a critical conversation

- Create a contract that outlines what we'll deliver, by when and at what cost, plus any expenses we will bill

- Assign a project

- List specific deliverables

- Give clear instructions

- Answer questions – clearly and completely

All these uses of email are flat-out critical for having good communication that builds strong, trusting relationships.

As a bonus, putting things in writing sends a message that we're detail-conscious and strengthens our reputation as a serious person with clear intentions for long-term success.

The first time — *anything!*

"I hope someone learns from my story," said Jason, a medical supplies vendor. "My first real account was a small division of a multi-national company. Almost immediately, the account started to grow as I got business from other parts of the company. Inside of a year, this one company was 80 percent of my business. The problem was that to get the account at first, I bid really low. I was making practically no money on my sales. After setting that precedent, I could never lose the label of 'cheapest and most qualified choice.'"

As Jason's business with this customer grew, so did his problem. The day came when he could no longer give them such low prices. "I was losing money, plus I knew I was being unfair to my other customers who were paying full price," he said. "I had to tell the client that my costs were going up across the board. They weren't happy, asked me to make an exception for them, then said they could no longer trust me. I lost all their business, but I survived, and I built a more diverse base of customers who pay a fair price for my products. It worked out okay, but I learned a big lesson. I'm just glad it didn't cost me my business."

When we're getting to know someone or settling into a new business situation, the precedents we set, that is, the initial agreements and any exceptions we make lay a foundation for relationships: how we will work together, what will be considered standard practice, and what others can expect from us. We may make an exception to get our foot in the door or spark a positive beginning, but especially early in a relationship, the other person has no way of knowing an exception from our standard operating procedure.

Result: in someone else's mind, the exceptions we make today are the expectations they have of us tomorrow.

Whether it's accepting an unrealistically low fee as in Jason's case or agreeing to a too-ambitious deadline, working on a weekend or holiday, doing something for free, or being willing to listen to a coworker who complains constantly, irresistible people know they have to set precedents with great care. They understand the powerful messages precedents send about how they work, the exceptions they're willing to make, and behaviors they'll accept.

When it comes to building irresistible levels of trust, this practice is essential. As we manage expectations people have of us by being careful about the exceptions we'll make and the favors we're willing to do, we ensure that others know what they can reasonably expect from us.

Result: no disappointments and irresistible trust!

Measure twice, cut once.

Irresistible people apply this "Carpenter's Rule" and pause before speaking to measure their words. This important theme of measuring words before they're said runs through much of irresistible people's careers. They think first about their listeners and are careful not to voice every idea and opinion. Instead, they determine in advance the issues, ideas, and information to share based on their listener's needs.

This is always important at work, but especially in tough situations when emotions are running high. Irresistible people protect their credibility and trustworthiness by reacting with objectivity and calm. Their thoughtful, measured responses garner lasting and well-deserved trust and respect from coworkers.

"Before I say anything, I always ask myself two questions," said one fast-tracked Managing Director at a health care company. "One: 'Is this honest and true?' and two: 'Will it lead to something positive?' If the answer to either question is no, I think long and hard before saying anything."

Homework
Listen to the difference between these two statements:

1) "They say it's dangerous not to drink enough water in the summer."

2) "A recent article in the *Times* explained that on a hot day, you can lose two quarts of water – the equivalent of four pounds – before you actually feel thirsty. By then you might be dangerously dehydrated."

The second statement carries much more weight and is more trustworthy. Information is just so much more authoritative and credible when it's supported by facts, comparative results, case stories, and precedents.

Irresistible people do their homework and present a balanced case for their ideas:

- How much will this save (cost)?

- What are the rewards (risks)?

- What is the most (least) favorable outcome we can expect?

Try this — what evidence might you offer to prove:

- The team needs two more people to handle its workflow.

- Everyone takes lunch at the same time leaving no one available to answer customer calls between 12 and 1 o'clock.

- The company's sales proposals need a refresh.

Ditch the hyperbole

- "She's absolutely brilliant, the most brilliant attorney I've ever met."

- "That guy? What a manager! He's definitely the best manager there ever was."

- "That was absolutely the worst conference ever."

- "She is completely impossible to work for."

Exaggeration like these statements hurts our credibility because it causes others to wonder about our judgment.

A situation or person is rarely all bad or all good. When exaggeration is a habit, our word becomes suspect. If instead, we ditch all forms of hyperbole, others are likely to conclude that what we're saying is believable and we're trustworthy.

As a plus, when we usually express our thoughts and opinions in a balanced way, when we do use the highest praise in a situation, it's taken seriously. We're not the kind of people who lavish unearned, empty flattery on everyone!

Mistake as lesson

Being willing to admit to mistakes, especially with the incredible power of good humor, is an amazing trust and credibility-building skill. Irresistible people know this intuitively. They regularly say things like, "Let me be responsible," "I missed that point; thanks for bringing it to my attention," and "You're right...let's try your idea instead." They accept responsibility for their mistakes and focus on learning from them, building high credibility in the process. As a bonus, they become even more human, likable...and trusted.

One Senior Editor of a large company magazine told the story of a pivotal moment in his leadership career. It centered on the time his team sent out 15,000 copies of the magazine with a typo that significantly misrepresented the payout from a new compensation program.

"My Managing Editor was literally shaking when she found the mistake. I knew this was a critical moment in her career. Was I going to let her have it? After all, this mistake would reflect badly on the whole team. But I felt like the best thing was to show her that it's not the mistake that matters, but how well and how fast we fix it. I gave her full latitude to fix the mistake and communicate the change."

This one discipline is evident in the careers of irresistible people across the board: the habit of being accountable when something goes wrong. When something doesn't go according to plan, irresistible people focus attention on the positive aspects of the situation, namely what went right (there's always something!) and what they'll do differently next time. People know they can be trusted to look forward, not back.

"

Trust is earned when actions meet words.

"

Be a people builder...

Give them support Encourage them always

Irresistible people consistently give others one of the rarest and most treasured of gifts: encouragement. They offer an honest boost when people need it, filling them with hope and a sense of possibility for the future. They empower others with positive, constructive thinking about their goals and challenges. In the process, they're relied on, sought after, and remembered in positive ways.

Encourage and be encouraged

"My mother told me to always offer
the next kid the bigger piece and
your piece would taste better."

– Barbara Corcoran

E veryone (and I do mean everyone!) needs support and encouragement, whether they admit it or not, and sometimes whether they're aware of it or not.

We're all so crazed and on edge with the pressures and responsibilities in our lives that when into the maelstrom speaks a positive, hopeful voice – we listen! Closely. At work, honest encouragement is like a multivitamin for our psyches and belief in our own potential. And because of all this, we think of the people who give it to us as, well, irresistible.

Irresistible people are irrepressible encouragers and people builders. They almost can't help themselves: they're determined that everyone – bosses, employees, customers, coworkers – will leave meetings and conversations with them feeling respected and valued. They leave winners in their wake, which means people want to be around them and are genuinely interested in their ideas and opinions.

They routinely give the credit away to others, complimenting their coworkers and teammates publicly and often. They talk about everyone in their circle in beneficial ways (which has the added benefit of casting a positive light on them as someone who is surrounded by positive, successful people).

Even the smallest act of encouragement at work — a simple, "That's a great question" or "I really like that idea"— can give someone a boost that lasts a long time. And when we're the person offering this encouragement, we'll be heard, genuinely liked, and on people's minds in positive ways in the future.

Importantly, real encouragement isn't patronizing people or just saying what we think they'd like to hear. It's not about puffing people up for no reason or cheering them on when they're doing something wrong. And it's not about being a pushover and gushing over every mediocre idea.

Real encouragement is finding ways to help people so that they walk away from us feeling valued, seeing their glass half full, and feeling supported when the going gets tough. It's having a healthy respect for our own influence, understanding how our everyday words and actions affect other people and being sure that effect is positive and constructive.

Real encouragement is being the go-to person when the going gets tough. In fact, genuine encouragement may be most valuable when things go sideways and get intense. Because that's when, instead of looking for a guilty party to point a finger at, irresistible people cover for others, show their faith in people by giving them the benefit of the doubt, and encourage them to create a better next time.

Let's get on this amazing irresistible career asset...

Irresistible encouragement

We are all influential

Each of us influences others, whether we're conscious of it or not. If we live on this planet and have contact with other humans, then our words, decisions, actions, and ideas affect the people around us.

It's helpful to think about the kind of influence we're having at work. Specifically, is it encouraging to be around us? To work with us? To work *for* us?

Irresistible people make others feel hopeful and positive. Coworkers leave meetings and conversations with them feeling energized and positive about the future. When something goes wrong, they react with strength and calm. In a conflict, they're the ones who can be counted on to look for a compromise — a way to support everyone while they make a tough situation better. And because of this, people look forward to talking to them. They feel safe confiding in them.

So who do you influence? Take a minute to think about how you'd finish these sentences:

"I influence [*people who work with and for me*]: _____."

"I indirectly influence [*people I interact with regularly at work*]: _____."

"Around me, people feel: _____."

"People know they can count on me to: _____."

"When something goes well, I'm the first person who: _____."

"When something goes wrong, I'm the first person who: _____."

If you're feeling courageous, you can ask a coworker you trust to answer these questions about you. Then compare answers to see what you can learn about how you're perceived and (maybe 😊) start making positive changes.

Picture the situation ahead

In our rush to get more done in less (and less) time, it can be tempting to talk without thinking: an offhand comment, an exhausted, "I don't have the energy to make this sound nice. I've just got to say it," or a blurted out, "That's a really bad idea." An abrupt "No" or "Are ya kidding?"

Tempting as this can be — and no matter how rushed or tired we are — we have to resist the urge! Irresistible people are so committed to being an encouraging voice at work that they never dismiss someone's ideas or give in to the impulse to say something regrettable, even when they're thinking:

"Seriously?"

"That's the most ridiculous thing I've ever heard."

"Sure...I'll believe that when I see it."

"There's literally nothing we can do about that."

Instead, they think before saying anything and then picture the situation (and their relationships with the people involved) a day or week or month from that moment if they just blurt out what's on their mind. Almost always, saying what's on their minds without thinking will just create problems, sometimes big ones.

If we're too rushed to think ahead in a balanced and encouraging way, we can buy some time: put the call on hold and take a few breaths before reacting. If it's a live conversation, we can just pause, breathe, and then answer with something like, "I need to [*talk to my team/think this through*]. Can I get back to you by Friday?" or "Sounds interesting...can we talk about it more at Wednesday's meeting?"

Great expectations

Irresistible people set high hopes. And — this is really important — they use these hopeful expectations to encourage people and bring about positive change in their lives and the lives of those around them.

Let's unpack this so we can follow their powerful model of encouragement and irresistibility...

Whether our expectations are optimistic or pessimistic, courageous or fearful, sensible or out of this world, they are definitely one thing: *gonna happen*. Our thoughts, actions, and choices are self-fulfilling. They'll attract positive experiences or negative ones...we actually get to decide.

When we get this simple truth, our work world opens up. Seriously.

What we expect is what we get for one clear reason:

Because it's what we're looking for.

Blue-sky

Positive, blue-sky expectations of good things to come put us in a good frame of mind: on the lookout for the people and work experiences that will fulfill those expectations. Good expectations keep frustration, disappointment, and discouragement at bay. In their place are clarity, respect, good communication, and high hopes — along with a healthy ability to take disappointment in stride because even on our toughest days at work, we expect better times to come — and they do.

As an example, if we choose to blame the company for the decision to shelve our project (it *was* personal!) and start to distrust our manager and withhold our best ideas, we'll be surrounded by negative energy that attracts conflict and controversy. Result: we may sour on other people's ideas because ours was dismissed. Why should they get any attention when we didn't? We may end up being overlooked for high potential assignments and promotions.

But if we "blue sky" the situation instead: we see our project getting shelved as a temporary setback and expect the project to be picked up again when the timing is better. We choose to learn more about why our project idea didn't fly right now and make improvements to our idea so it's better aligned with company strategy — and we can prove that it is. We believe (and one day we're right!) that we'll get a second chance to present the idea with its positive changes, much better and stronger, and with a better result.

We may be perfectly right to think that the client who never called us back after we gave him a great bargain just took advantage of us. But if we let ourselves believe that's "just the way it is," that all clients are hoping to cheat us, and we then start arming ourselves and relating to clients this way, our attitude and the mood around us will be defensive and difficult. Clients and prospects will respond by shying away because working with us is stressful and unappealing. We'll set ourselves up for a raft of frustrations, blaming and back and forth with customers...and plenty of conflict.

But if we "blue sky" the situation instead: we choose to expect – and beautiful someone, it is simply a choice – that something good will come out of the situation (the client may call us in the future; maybe he's already given our name to a colleague who plans to call us shortly; he genuinely appreciated the bargain we gave him and will give us more work in the future). Result: we literally begin to attract the circumstances that will make this happen.

Turnaround
So, if we expect problems...

"This project has been just awful, and this meeting's going to be another chapter in this nightmare."

"No matter what I say, Noah will never understand my side of this issue. It's not even worth trying."

"The vendor is trying to cheat us, but we can't let that happen. It's not worth trying to talk it out, let's just call the lawyers."

"Compromise with Jill? Seriously?"

...the negative voices in our lives will sound the loudest. So we'll pay attention to them, respond to them, spend our energy on them. Eventually, we'll find ourselves smack in the middle of controversy, dissent, and conflict:

The meeting will be the nightmare we're expecting.

145

Noah won't understand our perspective, the disagreement will deepen and may seep into other areas.

A lawsuit will set off a round of anger, recrimination, and fighting.

Our relationship with Jill will be contentious and unproductive.

If we instead turn things around through great expectations...

"It's been a tough project, but I'm expecting great things to come out of this meeting."

"I know I'll find the right words to help Noah understand my side of this issue."

"This contract dispute will work out. We just need to sit down and talk it through."

"I'm confident we can find a way to compromise with Jill so we can finish this work on time."

...the positive, healthful voices in our lives will sound the loudest. We'll pay attention to them and spend our energy on them. As a result, we'll look up and see harmony, opportunity, and encouraging results for us and everyone around us:

The meeting will go well and may even be a turning point that shifts the effort in a positive direction.

Noah will appreciate our perspective. We'll do the same for him, and our mutual respect will enable us to work together more effectively.

The contract dispute will be settled with both sides satisfied and the relationship intact.

A strong compromise with Jill will let us finish the work on schedule and set the stage for good collaboration in the future.

What a difference a positive change in our expectations makes in our ability to encourage people, and even ourselves in the bargain!

Hope-filled

Think of some of the best-selling inspirational books of all time:

- *As a Man Thinketh*, by James Allen

- *The Power of Positive Thinking*, by Norman Vincent Peale

- *The Seven Habits of Highly Effective People*, by Stephen Covey

Each of these books is in its zillionth publishing, translated into hundreds of languages.

What's the secret of their universal appeal and staying power?

One thing: the message of hope. (Personal detail: reading each of these books 20 times early in my life definitely sparked my own hope addiction ☺.)

These books tap into our deep desire for encouragement, for reasons to believe we can create a better future. Different books, different eras, different authors, one inspiring message. A hope-filled future is possible, which is nutrition for our sense of potential and belief in ourselves and in a brighter tomorrow.

This is the power and perennial appeal of a hope-filled look forward. It gives you strength, energy, and staying power to envision your breakthrough and see the race through to the end.

And we find the people who supply it to be in a word, *irresistible*.

This is why irresistible people tap into the power of encouraging people with a hope-filled look forward. They're the first to help everyone see a better future and suggest solutions for creating it.

They speak the language of encouragement:

- "You have great potential..."

- "I admire your sense of [*timing/vision/what makes people tick*]..."

- "I've got complete confidence in you."

- "You can't solve the entire problem right away, but I've got a few ideas that will help you in the short term."

- "Your idea doesn't sound far-fetched. In fact, I think it has potential. See how it plays out."

- "Anything is possible, and I think your solution is worth a try."

- "I know it's a lateral move instead of a promotion, but you'll be exposed to new material and work challenges. Then from there, who knows? I'm excited for you."

- "Hey, a mistake is better than never trying. Besides, you learned something for next time."

In the process, they give the people in their work lives strength, energy, and staying power to envision their next breakthrough and make it come alive. When we become irresistible – the person offering this kind of hope – we become an inspiration, a go-to when coworkers need advice or an idea, even (maybe especially) when the going gets rough.

No matter what someone is experiencing, nothing fortifies them like a positive, hope-filled look forward. In the moment, nothing but the words have changed, but the hope-filled and encouraging look forward changes literally *everything*. It lifts their mood, gives them a burst of energy, and puts them on the lookout for the people and experiences that will help them build a better future.

The question is the power
Questions shape our thoughts and actions for a simple reason: our brains are literally wired to immediately, reflexively focus on answering any question we're asked.

With this kind of power, we need to be exquisitely careful about the questions we ask. When these questions are negative and uninspiring...

"Why does this always have to happen?"

"Why is business so heartless?"

"Can't they just stop demanding so much from me?"

"Why doesn't he never just do it himself?"

...our minds are on the lookout for answers: "You know why this always happens? Because no one really cares" or "Because business is always just about the money" or "He won't do it himself because he's lazy, and btw, he'll take all the credit just the same."

Irresistible people understand the power of questions and use them to encourage others, keeping the mood upbeat, sparking new ideas, and framing opportunities and fresh starts:

"What do you think are your best opportunities right now?"

"How can we build on that idea?"

"How can we make it better next time, even just a little?"

"What steps can we take to solve this problem, and who can help us?"

"What can you do to make yourself even more marketable?"

Take a second to think about how great you feel when someone asks you questions like these and how irresistible you find that person!

More ideas for encouraging people in this way at work:

"What's been your best experience with..."

"If you could change this to the ideal situation/result, what would that be?"

"If you had a break in your day-to-day work and could fix anything around here, what would you tackle?"

"What was your favorite project last year?"

Language that empowers

Think about the difference between, "Don't take a break before 10 am," and "You can take a break after 10 am." It's the exact same message stated in positive terms, and it's so much easier to hear! It's also more respectful and empowering to the listener which means it's more likely to be heard and inspire action.

In fact, if there's one small change we can make right away that will have a big impact on our ability to encourage people, it may be using future-focused, open-ended language.

Like this:

Before	After
Neglected to	Need to
Lacks	Needs to include
Too hard for us	Will stretch our abilities
Struggle to	Strive to
Problem	Chance
Mistake	Opportunity
Deviates from	Needs to align with
Limited	Has room for growth
Overlooks	Needs to include
It won't be ready until after Tuesday.	It will be ready by Wednesday.
Don't forget...	Please remember...
You failed to sign the other copy.	Please sign the other copy.
You never call me.	I'm so glad to hear from you!

Again, all we have to do is picture how much better it feels to be on the receiving end of the **After** statements versus the **Before** statements!

The **Before** column shuts down conversation. Accusatory words like "overlooks," "lacks," and "struggle to" put people on the defensive, as do accusatory statements like, "You failed to sign the other copy" and "You never call me." Hearing these words, we feel guilty and defensive.

On the other hand, the language in the **After** column is forward-facing, affirming, and hopeful (there's a "chance/opportunity," "It will be ready," "Has room for growth"). This language also suggests positive action ("Please sign the other copy" and "Needs to include") and shows we have respect for the listener and high expectations for the situation. Irresistible people fill the workplace with hope-filled words like these that encourage and inspire everyone to take positive action.

A few simple ways to change from **Before** to **After** language:

Start thinking in terms of a future-focused "Next-time-let's" or "In-the-future-would-you..."

We can also think, "How can I say the same thing in the positive?" by telling someone what *to do* instead of what *not to do*, like when we tell our kids, "Hold the eggs carefully" rather than, "Don't drop the eggs!"

Rather than pulling up someone short for what they *haven't* done, we can thank them for what they have done as in, "I'm so you were able to make it!" instead of, "You never come to these meetings...why now?"

Then we can sit back and see just how much more comfortable, relaxed, and interested the people around us at work immediately become because of our irresistible encouragement!

"

*The secret of change is to focus
all of your energy not on fighting
the old, but on building the new.*

— Socrates

"

DIANA DAVIN

Solve problems...

Envision success
Be a catalyst for
positive change

Irresistible people tackle problems head on. They are the go-to people in tough situations who help others think ahead and envision success. And they empower everyone to take the right steps with confidence. They know that being someone who thinks in terms of solving problems is about as powerful as we can be at work.

A catalyst for positive change

"Problems are not stop signs.
They are guidelines."

– Robert H. Shuller

In today's work world, we're just not rewarded for doing what we're asked and nothing else. And that's good! It's hard to imagine us, with all our creativity and initiative and connectivity, and with so much to offer, marching around like robots doing little more than following orders.

Instead, we're expected to *apply* what we know: ask thoughtful questions, challenge conventional wisdom, and add strong ideas.

Irresistible people do all this and something more: they use what they know to make everyone and everything around them better. They are problem solvers, obstacle removers, and catalysts for positive change. In the face of a problem, they bring a calm head, which makes them especially irresistible in today's ultra-competitive, zero-margin-for-error, time-crunched world of work.

As a major plus, imagine how grateful people are when someone (us!) helps them solve their problems by asking great questions, searching for answers with them, and cheering them on.

This is what irresistible people know: when they think this way — when they operate as natural and reliable problem solvers — the people they work with and for don't have to. Irresistible people save them from having to worry about every idea, detail and next step...and no question: everyone around them appreciates that!

Time to get specific...

Irresistible
problem solving

Forward thinking

To solve problems, or even to be willing to try, irresistible people believe in the future, in possibilities, in their vision and the strength of their dreams. That boldness of belief in a better future energizes everyone around them.

Listen to what this sounds like, then can actively look for opportunities to follow their truly irresistible example:

"You know what's great about that idea?"

"We can make that even better. What if we..."

"Here's the upside..."

"I see a hidden win here."

"Let's think constructively about this for next time..."

"Here's what we can do in the future..."

"Let's try..."

"I think we're on the right track. Now, let's..."

"That's right, and..."

"We can do a lot with your idea."

Connect the dots
In the process of solving problems, irresistible people work hard to make information practical and usable for others. Rather than just providing raw data that requires their listeners to do a lot of work to understand and apply information, irresistible people offer context and examples of their ideas in action and interpret an important piece of information for the people around them.

This irresistible skill of "connecting the dots" may be one of the most important capabilities to master. People are hungry for help from sages who can help them make sense of it all, uncover the best information, test feasibility, and apply concepts quickly.

Irresistible people connect the dots for others by:

- Joining facts into meaningful connections ("Taken together, here's what all this means for us...")

- Interpreting information ("From these facts we can conclude...")

- Applying them ("Here's how these ideas would work for the next version of the website.")

- Making a reliable prediction ("Based on this information, we can safely say that in the future...")

- Solving a problem ("We can tell from this data that our concerns about an inventory shortage in Pasadena are unwarranted.")

Aha!
In response, their coworkers have an "Aha!" moment: they understand the facts (*what is*) and also how they can be used to

solve a problem, create a breakthrough, or help a project move ahead (*what can be*).

As they encourage everyone around them to solve problems and stretch beyond the obvious for something more, irresistible people know that connecting the dots isn't just a way of talking. It's a way of thinking and working that adds value to every situation, paving the way for:

Innovation: "This is how it works right now, but here's how I think we can make it better."

Initiative: "Let me take it from here and see how new customers would respond to this."

Turnarounds: "I've seen this happen a few times. It's part of the normal cycle this kind of program goes through. In fact, we saw the same drop in the numbers last year. Judging from my experience, it will rebound before January."

New solutions: "This unlocks an idea that I think has been staring us in the face, but we couldn't see because we've been so distracted by the problem."

Hope: "When we look at it with all the pieces together, the situation isn't as dire as we first thought." Or: "It may not look great at first glance, but I think there are other factors we can consider."

Not surprising then that connecting the dots for others does such a fantastic job of making us stand out as breakthrough-bound people at work who inspire everyone to look forward and work together.

It's not an exaggeration to say that this one practice may open more eyes (and more doors!) for us than any other concept, idea, or strategy.

As we build a reputation for adding value and insight to information, tying it all together, and using it to help people solve problems, our irresistibility soars.

What a relief to our already overworked and overburdened coworkers to realize they can do a little less thinking on this one because we've got it. We'll be doing the difficult job of thinking deeply about the problem, taking it a step further for everyone, and saving them the time and energy it would take to do this themselves.

"What if...?"

Irresistible people understand a key principle about tackling problems at work. These issues are often complex, and so solving them is hard! Irresistible people make themselves an asset in these situations by asking probing questions that are beyond the obvious to get to the deeper issues and help everyone think in terms of solutions.

So rather than face a problem by spending all their time studying what's happening now — what's causing the problem, who's responsible, how often this happens, when the problem started... — irresistible people get solution-oriented, wondering, "What if...?" and "What's next?" They think creatively about the steps they can take to streamline a process or make it work better in some other way. They involve other people and teams whose expertise will improve the quality of the work. And they search for better ways to accomplish just about anything.

Here's what this might sound like in practice:

"What if we include the Marketing team in the June meeting? They can probably tell us how to talk about the benefits of our idea to the Product Manager. Let's see if they're available."

"Let's find out how much we can save next year if we consolidate all our office supply purchases with one vendor. We'll start with a list of suppliers to consider."

"Last year, the client said she wished we had more time to plan the annual Sales Meeting. If we start a month earlier, we'll be able to plan more breakout discussions and maybe even include the European team and the Southern Region's digital content. Let's put a timeline together."

Flex these important muscles
Flexing our "What if?" as well as our "What's next?" problem-solving muscles makes us more valuable problem solvers and something more: it shows that we enjoy and are excited about what we do, believe that added quality matters, and are invested in the work and the success of the team or business. Who could resist all this?

Here are some questions to help us flex these important muscles:

- "What's the best result for our team or business? Are we doing everything we can to bring this about?"

- "How can we pick up momentum toward our goal? What steps can we take to:
  — save time or money?
  — create more energy and excitement for the goal?
  — get additional support from influential people?

- "What next steps would:
    - keep moving this effort along and make sure it doesn't stall?
    - show my manager/team/client/customer that I've got the long-term success of this program in sight?"

- "What is the client/customer likely to ask us to do next?"

- "Which teammates or colleagues would be willing/able to brainstorm next steps with us?"

- "Which executives can help us create interest by getting behind what we're trying to do?"

- "How are other teams or businesses treating this issue? What's working for them? How can we apply these ideas to the problem we're facing?"

- "Beyond what we have to do, what more can we do? What's the extra 2 percent we can do to take this effort from good to great?"

Possibilities!

When faced with a problem, irresistible people immediately think: possibilities! Problems and (more to the point) their solutions are loaded with positive potential: learning experiences, new connections, surprising strength, resiliency, and creativity.

Mistakes give us the opportunity to show how we handle challenges, adversity, and difficult situations. In the face of a mistake, irresistible people are calm and focused. They are creative in their approach to fixing the mistake, and they even do this with more energy and resolve than they did the original work. In the process, they get to showcase strengths that can't be visible any other way. They know that how we handle mistakes at work sends a powerful, memorable message about our focus, creativity, and commitment to getting it right.

How about customer complaints? Irresistible people aren't afraid or annoyed by complaints. They may not always love to hear them, but they want to because without complaints, there's no way to know why sales are declining or customers are leaving. More important, there's no way to know what needs to be improved to satisfy customers better.

Negative feedback? Same. Irresistible professionals want to hear it. Like customer complaints, they don't always love to hear it, but they *want* to because they know that's the only way to improve their performance in areas that matter to the people they work for. This is a quality of critical information they can't get any other way, and so they welcome it, and they treat it like the precious commodity and unique opportunity it is: the chance to improve.

Beautiful someone, it *does* take emotional strength to use this form of problem solving, but the benefits far outweigh the work involved. Luckily, there are tools – high potential questions – to help us brainstorm brand new possibilities: fresh solutions, new ideas, and surprising answers in the face of challenges:

Energizing questions
- "What result will let us walk away from this problem with a solid solution in place? What two steps can we take right now to set this in motion?"

- "A year from now, what three words would we like to come to mind when people talk about the results of our efforts to solve this problem today?"

Envisioning questions

- "What changes and trends do we see in the business world/our industry/our profession that excite us about the possibilities we'll unleash by solving this problem?"

- "What's been our best experience with something similar from the past that ended well? What ideas from that experience can we apply here?"

Imagining questions

- "If we had no limits (if we had unlimited money, time, and other resources), how could we handle this challenge?"

Connecting questions

- "How can we be sure everyone helping us knows how important they are to our success in solving this problem?"

- "Who are our champions? What two steps can we take to excite them about the potential of our goal here?"

"

Problems are nothing
but wake-up calls for creativity.

– Gerhard Gschwandtner

"

DIANA DAVIN

Smile more...

Be the "escape valve" when the going gets tough

There's something super-attractive about affable people. They're easy to be around. They know there's nothing like a good laugh — well timed — to clear the air and everyone's head.

They know how to make light of a tough situation, without being flip or inappropriate. They help others keep perspective, remember to laugh, and stay on track.

DIANA DAVIN

Keep perspective — remember to laugh

"If you could choose one characteristic
that would get you through life,
choose a sense of humor."

— Jennifer Jones

Have you ever worked with someone who exasperates everyone by being just too serious or easily upset? The wrong word, a certain look, an innocent question, an offhand comment, and they're annoyed, even indignant.

A sincere compliment is answered with, "With everything I do, *that's* what you appreciate?"

A simple request is greeted with a hyper-defensive: "I was out sick last week. How am I supposed to know the answer to that?" or "Cynthia said she would handle that, so I don't know anything about it."

What should be a momentary scuttle with a coworker becomes a full-scale war, "Who does he think he is, saying I should have made that call? That's *his* job! I can't work with him!"

How about someone who's so grim and focused that they're like the proverbial wet blanket in every situation, never willing to laugh or just let something go? They have a long memory for slights and annoyances, "Am I supposed to care what you think after what you said last year?"

177

Now, think about people who are just the opposite. In talking about them, we might say they're "approachable," "likable," and "easygoing." They are positive, pleasant people who see the bright side of every situation, are "a pleasure to work with" or "easy to do business with."

No matter what happens, they keep it in perspective and help everyone around them do the same. They seem to take even major problems in stride and calm everyone around them. They've got great perspective and can tell the difference between issues worth stressing about and momentary scuttles, mere hiccups.

Think about how naturally attractive these people are — how irresistible. Everyone knows they can be relied on for calm thinking, relaxed ways of handling tough situations at work, and positive, constructive ideas. They keep the mood light, and when appropriate, even help everyone see the humor in a situation to break the tension and lower the intensity.

At work, likable, easygoing people are irresistible because they're safe and comfortable to be around. They're not weak or passive, but rather people with strength under control who are smart and savvy enough to save their intensity for when it's truly warranted and will create a worthwhile result.

Escape valve

For just these reasons, one of the qualities irresistible people often share is a sense of humor. People feel, and rightly so, that they can go to their irresistible coworkers for relief, to lighten the mood, to somehow give them perspective, and make everything okay in the process.

And this is interesting: because of their balanced approach and unwillingness to take things too seriously or fly off the handle, they're considered more trustworthy. Since protests, arguments, and pessimism are not their usual style, when they choose to gripe or grumble in order to make a point, they're taken seriously rather than dismissed as someone who's always complaining.

At the same time, irresistible people have exquisite judgment about *when* to lighten the mood. For sure, it's not always appropriate as in the case of a serious mistake, expensive mishap, or difficult news. These are obvious examples, but there are other times when humor is not appropriate. When someone is genuinely upset or embarrassed or with superiors, humor can cross a line that could be impossible to return from.

Importantly, having a sense of humor is not about doing stand-up or being the center of attention as we tell jokes. It's the skill to help other people keep their perspective so they don't become exhausted by the ups and downs (especially the downs) of work life. Being able to chuckle at a situation releases tension, helps people remember to laugh (and remember that we *can* laugh) and keeps everyone on track, able to think clearly.

There's just nothing like a good laugh to clear the air and everyone's head. Imagine the relief we will bring coworkers and colleagues when we give them the perspective they're missing when they're upset. When we help them relax and know it will work out all right. When we help them not blow a given situation out of proportion by taking it too seriously.

We can build our own reputations for having this kind of light, easygoing style.

Here's how to start...

Irresistible perspective

First, be natural

If we want to instantly increase our personal appeal and irresistibility, we should be natural, just ourselves.

When we are natural, we relax, which makes other people relaxed around us. People also feel like they know us — the *real* us — and they're more comfortable and candid around us. They don't have to wonder if we have a secret agenda, who we really are or what we're really thinking. They know, or at least can make a pretty good guess. We're easy to be around, increasing the likelihood people will seek out our company, opinions and involvement.

Being natural is not about a loss of privacy or letting colleagues into your inner personal circle, but more a communication style that seems natural and feels more comfortable for everyone around you.

So, if outright humor comes naturally to you, if you're okay being the life of the party, go for it (within business limits!). Let that sense of humor shine through. If not, don't try to fake it. It will seem forced and phony. Instead, work at just injecting a lightness into your work and communication style. Relax, breathe, and be yourself.

Lower the intensity

After working with thousands of businesspeople, I've seen lots of choices they make, some super-successful, others not so much. I've watched people respond to work situations with gratitude, excitement, determination, frustration, and pride.

Some coworkers have been attracted to these behaviors, others have gotten angry at them, still others were motivated or intrigued.

But, beautiful someone, there's one reaction that everyone seems to find off-putting, and that is *intensity*.

Intensity is the superlative of any emotion.

So *anger* becomes *fury*.

Concern travels all the way across the spectrum to *terror*.

Interest becomes *obsession*.

Important becomes *do-or-die*.

Here's what intensity can sound like. In reaction to a simple comment or uncomplicated situation, intense people respond:

- "What's that supposed to mean?"

- "Even though he didn't say it, I'm sure he was talking about our team when he said *inefficiencies*."

- "I can't believe this total failure. What a mess! We'll never recover from this."

- "We can't just sit around and do nothing! We have to do something now!"

- "If it's not perfect, it's not good enough for me."

- "They didn't like it. We should just forget it. They're impossible to please."

- "I don't think that's a laughing matter. I don't know why you'd find that funny."

So much drama! And everyone (understandably) wants to run fast in the opposite direction.

Too much

Intense people are stubborn and inflexible and have a fragile ego that prevents them from accepting anything but the most glowing feedback. They tend to speak in superlatives (things are "great" or "awful," never anything in between).

At work, this is all just too much, and it's easy to see why. Our best work vibe is controlled, focused, and strong. Intensity is furthest thing from every one of these qualities. It evinces over-the-top seriousness, plus a lack of perspective: not qualities that scream upward mobility on the job. Intense people tend to be dour and unwilling to laugh at themselves — or sometimes to laugh at all — often compounded by hypersensitivity and super-annoying amounts of self-concern.

All this drama is just exhausting to be around, making intensity the literal opposite of irresistible. So rather than be drawn to them, coworkers react to the over-the-topness by backing up a few steps and eventually doing everything possible to avoid them.

Quick caveat: intensity can be important at times. Critical calculations that are wrong. Mistakes in logic that could cost the team or business in significant ways. Research findings that indicate urgent action is needed.

In these situations, we need to apply some solid judgment: is the situation or outcome truly critical? Does it deserve exceptional attention and energy? If yes, some well-placed intensity is appropriate. And as a bonus, when we're usually calm and balanced, using our intensity sparingly, we're taken seriously when we do raise the temperature on a situation instead of dismissed as someone who's just dramatic about everything!

Lighter

Irresistible people make it a practice to lower the intensity and lighten the mood.

So whenever you feel the impulse to react in a less than resourceful way to a tough situation — take a break. Go for a walk, make a call, listen to a favorite track — do anything to put space between the situation and your reaction. Spend some time processing what's going on and the effect your reaction may have on the people around you.

Err on the side of giving people the benefit of the doubt. Everyone can have a bad day, week, or even month. There's also the possibility that whatever is upsetting you was unintentional: "I don't believe she meant any harm. She just forgot to call, that's all. I've done it a hundred times myself!"

And definitely: let's cut ourselves some slack! We don't need to be perfect 24/7 and remembering this lowers our own intensity.

It can be hard to keep this in mind, but no one's thinking about us the way we are. Most people are so busy with their own needs and concerns that they aren't focused on us as often as we may think.

Remembering all this, we can keep the mood light and let go of an issue because our ongoing focus on it will only increase everyone else's. By bringing it up or justifying it, we're keeping it in the spotlight. (They've forgotten...honestly, they have.)

Drop it

Into every work life, some rain will fall. That's a reality we can all embrace intellectually, but it's easy to get caught up, distracted by inevitable scuffs and bruises and lose focus on the goals, projects, and people that really matter. Upset that someone's actions have stalled our progress on an important project or maybe an unpredictable event that made us look bad, we lose perspective and get more frustrated by the minute.

Irresistible people are ready for these times. They keep it light and encourage everyone around them with reminders of how well things worked out last time something like this happened. They remember a forgiving coworker who overlooked a mistake they made with a smile and a light, "No worries!" or a manager who took problems in stride and inspired everyone to keep moving ahead, carrying only lessons learned, not the bumps and bruises from the mistake itself. They just drop it so they can look ahead, and they encourage everyone on the team to do the same. They look steady and calm, just the kind of irresistible professional everyone wants to be around.

Following this example, we can all remember a time when we decided to drop something, however large or small, and the literal lightness and relief we felt. This is because grudges are physical burdens we carry, a virtual suitcase of bricks. All they do is slow us down and hurt our reputation as a breakthrough-bound person who's easy to work with and professional enough to stay focused on the future. Grudges are career stoppers for sure. They make us look too serious, plus inexperienced and incapable of handling our emotions at work effectively.

So let's use this to boost our own irresistibility. Whatever the issue, think about it carefully: will you look positive and strong by rehashing something in order to defend yourself, or be much more powerful by just dropping it and moving on? Choosing the second option, you'll look like the rock star you are, above the nonsense and not even a little unsettled by the situation. You'll make any changes needed, and cartwheel right out of it.

Rather than let mistakes and rough spots ruffle you, encourage everyone to roll with them with an easy-going, "Hey, it's no problem," "Sure thing," "You got it," "No big deal!" or "Let's not sweat this one." Think of the boost your reputation for being a calm, focused professional will get and also how you'll strengthen our image as a breakthrough-bound person with good perspective whose emotions are under control and who can tell a real issue from a momentary squabble.

Humble

How cringy is it to be around someone who constantly brags about their virtues — their food choices, workouts, work ethic, accomplishments — in general flaunting their standards and achievements?

All this telegraphs a brand of self-righteousness that makes other people feel either really uncomfortable or really competitive. This behavior also shows a level of intensity about their standards and a lack of humility that make others feel judged as somehow inferior.

Irresistible people don't lower their standards to make other people feel comfortable, they just keep the mood light by keeping them to themselves. They do what their standards dictate, without self-righteously announcing their reasons for making the choices they do. They know that at their best, standards aren't for bragging about; they're for living out based on decisions they've made about what's right for them in their lives and careers.

And if they want to inspire others, they know the best way to do that is to simply live out their standards. Their wordless example is so much more motivating to others than anything they might loudly declare. Other people witness their actions and decide for themselves, a way of operating that also shows deep respect for other people's choices and decision-making process.

Impossible to offend

Think of how powerful — in addition to irresistible — we are when we are literally impossible to offend. Nothing, not even a direct and deliberate insult, anyone says or does gets under our skin to irritate or anger us.

And when we put it into practice every day, what a difference it makes in our lives and careers. How much more relaxed and focused on the kinds of things that move us forward rather than on the hundreds of truly insignificant things that happen every day to annoy and distract us. How much better at calm listening. How much more likeable and easier to be around. How much stronger our reputation for being a positive touchstone with great perspective.

And when we do get genuinely upset, how much more seriously we're taken because we're not blown off as someone who's always running around, hair on fire.

Let's try this for an instant power surge in our work lives: be quick to listen, slow to speak...and impossible to offend!

"

Finish every day and be done with it.
You have done what you could;
some blunders and absurdities crept in;
forget them as soon as you can.
Tomorrow is a new day.
You shall begin it serenely and with
too high a spirit to be encumbered
with your old nonsense.

— Ralph Waldo Emerson

"

DIANA DAVIN

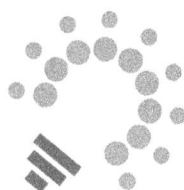

That's all for now!

S ufi poet Rumi wrote that he believed, "Yesterday I was clever, so I wanted to change the world. Today I am wise, so I am changing myself."

My wish for us, beautiful someone, is that we understand this important truth and bring it to all aspects of our lives with equal force and belief.

At work especially, with so many forces coming at us, let's remember that change is always an inside out process – it starts with us. Knowing this, we can set out together on a positive journey that attracts the best of everything to us and everyone around us.

And as always, if there was anything in *Simply Irresistible* that you found especially helpful, please share it with someone you care about. My hope is that my books bless many more people than I will ever know.

I wish you only good things,

Diana